CFA Institute

GLOBAL ESG DISCLOSURE STANDARDS FOR INVESTMENT PRODUCTS HANDBOOK

June 2022

ISBN 978-1-956563-02-3
eISBN 978-1-956563-03-0

ABOUT THE HANDBOOK

The Global ESG Disclosure Standards for Investment Products and this Handbook were created with the assistance of the ESG Technical Committee and the predecessor ESG Working Group. We are very grateful to these volunteers for their time and efforts. We also appreciate the individuals and organizations that reviewed drafts of these documents and provided comments and input.

ESG Technical Committee

Bruno Bertocci, Chair
UBS Asset Management (retired)
USA

Toby Belsom
PRI
United Kingdom

Jeroen Bos, CFA
Credit Suisse Asset Management
The Netherlands

Emily Chew
Calvert Research and Management
USA

Chris Fidler
CFA Institute
USA

Madhu Gayer, CIPM
Singapore

Barry Gladstein, CFA
Macquarie Asset Management
USA

Martin Jarzebowski, CFA
Federated Hermes
USA

Christoph Klein, CFA
ESG Portfolio Management
Germany

Linda-Eling Lee, Ph.D.
MSCI
USA

Na Li, CFA
National Council for Social Security Fund (NCSS)
China

Vhahangwele Manavhela
Aequalitas Capital Partners
South Africa

Brian Minns, CFA
University Pension Plan
Canada

Jason Mitchell
Man Group
United Kingdom

Kanol Pal, CFA
BNP Paribas Wealth Management
Singapore

Erika Spence
eVestment, A Part of Nasdaq
USA

Stephanie Li Ying Teh, CFA
State Street Global Advisors
Australia

Nathalie Wallace
Natixis Investment Managers
USA

Reinhilde Weidacher
Institutional Shareholder Services
Sweden

ESG Working Group

Toby Belsom
PRI
United Kingdom

Bruno Bertocci
UBS Asset Management (retired)
USA

Jeroen Bos, CFA
Credit Suisse Asset Management
Switzerland

Ulrika Hasselgren
Coeli Group
Sweden

Brian Henderson, Ph.D.
Mercer
United Kingdom

Daniel Ingram
Wilshire
USA

Linda-Eling Lee, Ph.D.
MSCI
USA

Christopher Merker, Ph.D., CFA
Baird
USA

Alberto Estévez Olleros, CFA
Santander Asset Management
Spain

Kanol Pal, CFA
BNP Paribas Wealth Management
Singapore

Elena Philipova
London Stock Exchange Group
Switzerland

Alexis Rosenblum, CFA
BlackRock
USA

Hardik Shah, CFA
GMO LLC
Singapore

Adela Skenderasi, CFA
Brown Advisory
USA

Roger Urwin
Willis Towers Watson
United Kingdom

CFA Institute Staff

Chris Fidler
Deborah Kidd, CFA
David Terris, CIPM
Karyn Vincent, CFA, CIPM
Robin Willis

Consultant

Ann Putallaz, Ph.D., CIPM
AFP Consulting, LLC

CONTENTS

The Global ESG Disclosure Standards for Investment Products 1

Preface 1

Introduction 3

Guiding Principles for Investment Product ESG Disclosures 5

1. Fundamentals of Compliance 6

2. Investment Product ESG Disclosures 8

3. ESG Terminology 13

Glossary 18

Appendix A: Determining the Applicability of Provisions 21

Appendix B: Sample ESG Disclosure Statements 25

Appendix C: Development of the Global ESG Disclosure Standards for Investment Products 40

Appendix D: Relationship to Regulations and Other Codes and Standards 42

Errata for the Global ESG Disclosure Standards for Investment Products 45

Explanation of the Provisions of the Global ESG Disclosure Standards for Investment Products 47

Introduction 47

1. Fundamentals of Compliance 48

2. Investment Product ESG Disclosures 59

3. ESG Terminology 115

Errata for the Explanation of the Provisions of the Global ESG Disclosure Standards for Investment Products 123

PL Qualified Activity CFA Institute

This publication qualifies for 4 PL credits, including 4 SER credits, under the guidelines of the CFA Institute Professional Learning Program.

THE GLOBAL ESG DISCLOSURE STANDARDS FOR INVESTMENT PRODUCTS

PREFACE

All investors have needs and preferences that can be defined in terms of risk tolerance, return objectives, time horizon, and liquidity. A significant number of investors, however, also have needs and preferences that relate to ESG issues. Investors' motivations related to ESG issues vary greatly. Some of the more common motivations stem from a desire to:

- incorporate ethical principles, values, or religious beliefs into investment decisions;
- avoid ESG risks that may negatively affect the value of investments;
- mitigate the negative impacts of investments on the environment and other people; and
- contribute, wholly or partially, to the attainment of specific, positive, measurable environmental or social outcomes.

In response to investors' interest in ESG issues, the investment management industry has developed a variety of approaches for considering ESG issues in an investment product's objectives, investment process, or stewardship activities. More than one ESG approach can be used in a single investment product, and ESG approaches can be used in different ways and to address different ESG issues. As a result, a wide variety of investment products that consider ESG issues are available in the marketplace, and it is very difficult to sort these products into well-defined categories.

In addition, the terminology associated with incorporating ESG approaches into investment products is not standardized. It is not uncommon to see the same term referring to different ESG approaches or types of investment products—or to see different terms referring to the same ESG approach or type of investment products.

The confluence of the aforementioned factors has resulted in an increase in "greenwashing"—that is, a situation in which disclosures or advertising materials intentionally or inadvertently mislead investors about the ESG approaches used in an investment product, the ESG characteristics of an investment product, or the degree of influence that an investment product has on ESG issues. Over time, greenwashing may lead to an erosion of trust in the investment management industry.

The problems of overlapping investment product categorization, non-standardized terminology, and greenwashing are unlikely to be fully addressed by a single solution. Multiple, mutually reinforcing solutions are required if these problems are to be addressed in all markets around the world and for all types of investment products. Regulation is, and will continue to be, a powerful tool. However, educational programs, such as the CFA Institute Certificate in ESG Investing, and industry standards, such as the Global ESG Disclosure Standards for Investment Products, have important roles to play as well.

INTRODUCTION

CFA Institute is a not-for-profit association of investment professionals with the mission of leading the investment profession globally by promoting the highest standards of ethics, education, and professional excellence for the ultimate benefit of society.

The Global ESG Disclosure Standards for Investment Products (the "Standards") are ethical standards based on the principles of fair representation and full disclosure. They are designed to communicate information about an investment product's consideration of environmental, social, and governance (ESG) issues in its objectives, investment process, or stewardship activities.

The Standards use the term "ESG" as a descriptor to distinguish information, issues, and approaches that are connected in some form to the environment, society, and corporate governance from information, issues, and approaches that are not. The Standards do not use the term "ESG" as a descriptor to distinguish among different types of investment products, nor do they offer any criteria or guidance for what is or is not an "ESG investment product."

The Standards use the term "ESG approach" to refer to any one of a variety of methods for considering ESG issues in an investment product's objectives, investment process, or stewardship activities. This term includes but is not limited to approaches that are often referred to as ESG integration, exclusion, screening, best-in-class, thematic, sustainability themed investing, impact investing, and stewardship.

The Standards use the term "ESG Disclosure Statement" to refer to a document that contains, at a minimum, all of the required disclosures that apply to a specific-investment product.

Purpose and Scope

The purpose of the Global ESG Disclosure Standards for Investment Products is to facilitate fair representation and full disclosure of an investment product's consideration of ESG issues in its objectives, investment process, or stewardship activities. When investment products' ESG approaches are fairly represented and fully disclosed, investors, consultants, advisors, and distributors can better understand, evaluate, and compare investment products, and the potential for greenwashing diminishes.

The scope of the Global ESG Disclosure Standards for Investment Products focuses narrowly on disclosure of the ESG approaches used in an investment product. The Standards do not address:

- corporate ESG reporting,
- firm-level ESG disclosures (with an exception related to stewardship activities),

- naming, labeling, or rating of investment products, or
- the content of investment products' periodic reports.

The Standards are "global" in that they have been designed to accommodate:

- all types of investment vehicles—including but not limited to pooled funds, exchange-traded funds (ETFs), strategies for separately managed accounts, limited partnerships, and insurance-based investment products;
- all asset classes—including but not limited to listed equities, fixed income, private equity, private debt, infrastructure, and real estate;
- all ESG approaches—including but not limited to ESG integration, exclusion, screening, best-in-class, thematic, sustainability themed investing, impact investing, and stewardship;
- active and passive strategies; and
- all markets.

Compliance and Independent Assurance

Compliance with the Global ESG Disclosure Standards for Investment Products is voluntary. An investment manager may choose the investment products to which it applies the Standards. An investment manager must take all steps necessary to ensure that it has satisfied all the applicable requirements of the Standards before claiming that an ESG Disclosure Statement complies with the Standards. Implementing adequate internal controls instills confidence in the validity of disclosures as well as the claim of compliance.

An investment manager may choose to have an independent third party provide assurance for one or more of its ESG Disclosure Statements. All requirements and recommendations (other than Provision 1.B.1) for both investment managers and firms conducting assurance engagements will appear in separate assurance procedures for the Global ESG Disclosure Standards for Investment Products.

GUIDING PRINCIPLES FOR INVESTMENT PRODUCT ESG DISCLOSURES

The Global ESG Disclosure Standards for Investment Products are based on the principles of fair representation and full disclosure. When these principles are applied to investment product ESG disclosures, investors are provided with information that is:

- Complete.

  Investment product ESG disclosures fully disclose information that investors need in order to understand the investment product's ESG approaches. Significant information is not omitted.
- Reliable.

  Investment product ESG disclosures fairly represent the investment product's ESG approaches. Investment product ESG disclosures are not false or misleading.
- Consistent.

  Investment product ESG disclosures agree with, and supplement, regulatory disclosures and marketing materials.
- Clear.

  Investment product ESG disclosures are sufficiently specific and precise to effectively communicate to investors the investment product's ESG approaches.
- Accessible.

  Investment product ESG disclosures are readily available to investors.

1. FUNDAMENTALS OF COMPLIANCE

A. Fundamentals of Compliance—Requirements

1.A.1 The INVESTMENT MANAGER MUST comply with any laws and regulations that apply to the preparation and distribution of an ESG DISCLOSURE STATEMENT.

1.A.2 The INVESTMENT MANAGER MUST comply with all REQUIREMENTS of the Global ESG Disclosure Standards for Investment Products, including any INTERPRETIVE GUIDANCE, that apply to a specific INVESTMENT PRODUCT in order to state that the ESG DISCLOSURE STATEMENT for that specific INVESTMENT PRODUCT has been prepared and presented in compliance with the Global ESG Disclosure Standards for Investment Products.

1.A.3 An INVESTMENT MANAGER MUST NOT represent or state that an ESG DISCLOSURE STATEMENT is "in compliance with the Global ESG Disclosure Standards for Investment Products except for…" or make any other statements that may indicate partial compliance with the Global ESG Disclosure Standards for Investment Products.

1.A.4 The INVESTMENT MANAGER MUST NOT, in an ESG DISCLOSURE STATEMENT:

a. present information that is false or misleading;

b. omit significant information about the INVESTMENT PRODUCT'S ESG APPROACHES; or

c. contradict disclosures made in the INVESTMENT PRODUCT'S regulatory documents.

1.A.5 The ESG DISCLOSURE STATEMENT MUST cover a minimum period of one year, or the period since inception if the INVESTMENT PRODUCT has existed for less than one year.

1.A.6 The INVESTMENT MANAGER MUST document its policies and procedures for:

a. establishing and maintaining compliance with the REQUIREMENTS of the Global ESG Disclosure Standards for Investment Products, as well as any RECOMMENDATIONS it has chosen to adopt; and

b. monitoring and identifying changes and additions to the Global ESG Disclosure Standards for Investment Products and INTERPRETIVE GUIDANCE.

1.A.7 The INVESTMENT MANAGER MUST capture and maintain documents and records necessary to support the information included in an ESG DISCLOSURE STATEMENT.

1.A.8 The INVESTMENT MANAGER MUST notify CFA Institute of its use of the Global ESG Disclosure Standards for Investment Products by submitting the ESG STANDARDS COMPLIANCE NOTIFICATION FORM. This form MUST be filed:

a. when the INVESTMENT MANAGER initially completes an ESG DISCLOSURE STATEMENT for any one of its INVESTMENT PRODUCTS; and

b. thereafter annually between 1 January and 30 June.

1.A.9 If the INVESTMENT MANAGER chooses to apply the Global ESG Disclosure Standards for Investment Products to a specific INVESTMENT PRODUCT, the INVESTMENT MANAGER MUST make the ESG DISCLOSURE STATEMENT for that specific INVESTMENT PRODUCT available to INVESTORS.

1.A.10 The INVESTMENT MANAGER MUST update an INVESTMENT PRODUCT'S ESG DISCLOSURE STATEMENT when:

- **a.** changes are made to applicable Global ESG Disclosure Standards for Investment Products REQUIREMENTS or INTERPRETIVE GUIDANCE;
- **b.** the INVESTMENT MANAGER makes changes that affect information included in an ESG DISCLOSURE STATEMENT; or
- **c.** a significant error is found after the ESG DISCLOSURE STATEMENT is made available to INVESTORS.

B. Fundamentals of Compliance—Recommendations

1.B.1 The INVESTMENT MANAGER SHOULD obtain independent assurance on its ESG DISCLOSURE STATEMENTS.[1]

[1]See the Introduction for additional information about compliance and independent assurance.

2. INVESTMENT PRODUCT ESG DISCLOSURES

A. Investment Product ESG Disclosures—Requirements

General

2.A.1 If the INVESTMENT MANAGER chooses to apply the Global ESG Disclosure Standards for Investment Products to a specific INVESTMENT PRODUCT, the INVESTMENT MANAGER MUST prepare an ESG DISCLOSURE STATEMENT for that specific INVESTMENT PRODUCT that includes:

a. the name of the INVESTMENT PRODUCT;

b. the name of the INVESTMENT MANAGER;

c. the applicable disclosures REQUIRED by the Global ESG Disclosure Standards for Investment Products, except for any disclosures prohibited by law or regulation;

d. the period covered by the ESG DISCLOSURE STATEMENT;

e. a description of any changes made during the period covered by the ESG DISCLOSURE STATEMENT that are relevant to the applicable disclosures REQUIRED by the Global ESG Disclosure Standards for Investment Products, along with the effective dates of those changes;

f. a description of any changes made to the ESG DISCLOSURE STATEMENT within the past year to correct a significant error; and

g. the following statement:

> "This ESG Disclosure Statement for [Insert period covered by the ESG DISCLOSURE STATEMENT] complies with the disclosure requirements of the Global ESG Disclosure Standards for Investment Products. Additionally, [Insert name of INVESTMENT MANAGER] has complied with the requirements of the Global ESG Disclosure Standards for Investment Products related to the preparation and presentation of this ESG Disclosure Statement.
>
> The Global ESG Disclosure Standards for Investment Products are developed and maintained by CFA Institute. CFA Institute does not endorse or promote this organization, nor does it warrant the accuracy or quality of the content contained herein."

2.A.2 If an INVESTMENT MANAGER is prohibited by law or regulation from making a REQUIRED disclosure in the ESG DISCLOSURE STATEMENT, then the INVESTMENT MANAGER MUST disclose a description of the REQUIRED disclosure that cannot be included and explain why it cannot be included.

2.A.3 The INVESTMENT MANAGER MUST disclose a summary description of the ESG APPROACHES used in the INVESTMENT PRODUCT.

2.A.4 If the INVESTMENT PRODUCT'S investment process, STEWARDSHIP ACTIVITIES, or objectives systematically address one or more specific ESG issues, then the INVESTMENT MANAGER MUST disclose a summary description of those specific ESG issues.

2.A.5 The INVESTMENT MANAGER MUST disclose any third-party ESG-related labels and certifications with which the INVESTMENT PRODUCT complies.

Sources and Types of ESG Information

2.A.6 If ESG information is used in an INVESTMENT PRODUCT'S investment process or STEWARDSHIP ACTIVITIES, then the INVESTMENT MANAGER MUST disclose:

a. the elements of the investment process or STEWARDSHIP ACTIVITIES that use ESG information and how the ESG information is used;

b. a description of the type of ESG information used and a description of the sources from which that ESG information is obtained; and

c. the risks and limitations of the ESG information used and how those risks and limitations are managed.

Systematic Consideration of Financially Material ESG Information in Investment Decisions

2.A.7 If financially material ESG information is systematically considered in investment decisions, then the INVESTMENT MANAGER MUST disclose:

a. how financially material ESG information is typically identified;

b. how financially material ESG information is typically incorporated into investment decisions, differentiated by type of investment when necessary; and

c. exceptions in which financially material ESG information is not considered in investment decisions, if any.

ESG Investment Universe

2.A.8 If the INVESTMENT PRODUCT uses an ESG INDEX as an investment universe, then the INVESTMENT MANAGER MUST disclose:

a. either the significant ESG characteristics of the index or, if the index is a readily recognized index, the name of the index; and

b. how an INVESTOR can obtain information about the index construction methodology.

Screening

2.A.9 If an INVESTMENT PRODUCT has criteria that systematically exclude certain investments or has criteria that need to be met in order for an investment to be considered for inclusion in the portfolio, then the INVESTMENT MANAGER MUST disclose for each criterion:

a. the characteristic of the investment that is evaluated;

b. the threshold or condition against which the characteristic is compared;

c. whether the investment is excluded from, or is eligible for inclusion in, the portfolio when the threshold or condition is met; and

d. a reference, where applicable, to any law, regulation, or third-party standard, guideline, or framework used in the establishment or evaluation of the criterion.

2.A.10 If an INVESTMENT PRODUCT has criteria that systematically exclude certain investments or has criteria that need to be met in order for an investment to be considered for inclusion in the portfolio, then the INVESTMENT MANAGER MUST disclose:

a. where the criteria are applied in the investment process; and

b. the exceptions to the application of the criteria, if any.

Portfolio-Level ESG Characteristics

2.A.11 If the INVESTMENT PRODUCT has targets for portfolio-level ESG characteristics, then the INVESTMENT MANAGER MUST disclose for each target:

a. the portfolio-level ESG characteristic that is evaluated;

b. how the portfolio-level ESG characteristic is measured;

c. the target value or range for the portfolio-level ESG characteristic;

d. how the target portfolio-level ESG characteristic is expected to be attained;

e. the risks that could significantly hinder the attainment of the target portfolio-level ESG characteristic, should they occur; and

f. a reference, where applicable, to any law, regulation, or third-party standard, guideline, or framework used to measure the portfolio-level ESG characteristic or set the target.

2.A.12 If the INVESTMENT PRODUCT uses an ESG INDEX as a point of comparison for portfolio-level ESG characteristics, then the INVESTMENT MANAGER MUST disclose:

a. the portfolio-level ESG characteristics that are compared with the ESG INDEX;

b. either the significant ESG characteristics of the ESG INDEX or, if the ESG INDEX is a readily recognized index, the name of the ESG INDEX; and

c. how an INVESTOR can obtain information about the definitions of and calculation methodologies for the ESG characteristics of the ESG INDEX.

2.A.13 If the INVESTMENT PRODUCT has targets for portfolio-level ESG characteristics, then the INVESTMENT MANAGER MUST disclose how progress toward, or attainment of, those targets is reported to INVESTORS.

Portfolio-Level Allocation Targets

2.A.14 If the INVESTMENT PRODUCT has portfolio-level allocation targets for investments that have specific ESG characteristics, then the INVESTMENT MANAGER MUST disclose for each allocation target:

- **a.** the specific ESG characteristics of the investments for which there is an allocation target; and
- **b.** the allocation target value or range.

2.A.15 If the INVESTMENT PRODUCT has portfolio-level allocation targets for investments that have specific ESG characteristics, then the INVESTMENT MANAGER MUST disclose how progress toward, or attainment of, those targets is reported to INVESTORS.

Stewardship Activities

2.A.16 The INVESTMENT MANAGER MUST disclose how an INVESTOR can obtain a complete and current copy of all of the policies that govern the INVESTMENT PRODUCT'S STEWARDSHIP ACTIVITIES.

2.A.17 If ESG issues are typically considered when undertaking STEWARDSHIP ACTIVITIES, the INVESTMENT MANAGER MUST disclose:

- **a.** the types of STEWARDSHIP ACTIVITIES typically undertaken for the INVESTMENT PRODUCT, differentiated by type of investment where necessary;
- **b.** the ESG issues typically considered when undertaking those STEWARDSHIP ACTIVITIES;
- **c.** how those STEWARDSHIP ACTIVITIES and ESG issues are relevant to the INVESTMENT PRODUCT'S objectives and investment process; and
- **d.** the processes and systems that support the STEWARDSHIP ACTIVITIES undertaken for the INVESTMENT PRODUCT.

2.A.18 The INVESTMENT MANAGER MUST disclose how STEWARDSHIP ACTIVITIES for the INVESTMENT PRODUCT are reported to INVESTORS.

Environmental and Social Impact Objectives

2.A.19 If investments are made with the intention to generate positive, measurable SOCIAL and ENVIRONMENTAL impact alongside a financial return, then the INVESTMENT MANAGER MUST disclose:

a. the impact objectives in measurable or observable terms;

b. the stakeholders who will benefit from the attainment of the impact objectives;

c. the time horizon over which the impact objectives are expected to be attained;

d. how the impact objectives are related to other objectives that the INVESTMENT PRODUCT has and how the pursuit of the impact objectives could result in trade-offs with those other objectives;

e. how the attainment of the impact objectives will contribute to third-party sustainable development goals, if there is a stated intention to do so;

f. the proportion of the portfolio committed to generating SOCIAL and ENVIRONMENTAL impact;

g. how the impact objectives are expected to be attained;

h. the risks that could significantly hinder the attainment of the impact objectives, should they occur;

i. how progress toward, or attainment of, the impact objectives is measured, monitored, and evaluated;

j. how progress toward the attainment of the impact objectives is reported to INVESTORS; and

k. the process for assessing, addressing, monitoring, and managing potential negative SOCIAL and ENVIRONMENTAL impacts that may occur in the course of attaining the impact objectives.

B. Investment Product ESG Disclosures—Recommendations

[None]

3. ESG TERMINOLOGY

ESG terminology is often a barrier to investors' understanding of the ESG approaches used in an investment product. Sometimes, investment managers use technical terms that are understood within the investment management industry but are unfamiliar to the average investor. Other times, investment managers use words that have a commonly understood meaning but carry a special meaning when used in the context of ESG investing.

To avoid confusion, an investment manager's best course of action may be to describe its investment products' ESG approaches in plain language whenever possible. Sometimes, however, it is helpful to use a specialized term in place of a long phrase. When using a specialized term whose meaning may be unfamiliar to the reader, it is best practice to define the term the first time it is used.

To help investment managers prepare ESG disclosures that are clear to investors, this section includes references for the terms and definitions that tend to cause the most confusion. Following the references are recommendations that apply specifically to the preparation of ESG Disclosure Statements. Investment managers might also choose to follow these recommendations when preparing regulatory disclosures and marketing materials—provided that doing so would not violate any law or regulation.

Although this section is generally organized around various ESG approaches, it should not be assumed that the ESG approaches referred to in this section constitute an exhaustive list of all ESG approaches. Additionally, it should not be assumed that the following ESG approaches are mutually exclusive. An investment product can incorporate more than one ESG approach.

A. ESG Terminology—Requirements

[None]

B. ESG Terminology—Recommendations

ESG Integration

References

> "**ESG integration:** The inclusion of ESG considerations within financial analysis and investment decisions. This may be done in various ways, tailored to the investment style and approach of the fund manager."
>
> —CFA Institute, "Certificate in ESG Investing: Official Training Manual," 3rd Edition, 2021

"**ESG integration:** The process of including ESG factors in investment analysis and decisions to better manage risks and improve returns. It is often used in combination with screening and thematic investing."

—PRI, "Reporting Framework Glossary," 2021

"**ESG integration:** The systematic and explicit inclusion by investment managers of environmental, social and governance factors into financial analysis."

—Global Sustainable Investment Alliance (GSIA), "Global Sustainable Investment Review 2020," 2020

3.B.1 The INVESTMENT MANAGER SHOULD use the term "ESG integration" in a manner consistent with the previously referenced definitions.

3.B.2 The INVESTMENT MANAGER SHOULD provide a definition for the term "ESG integration" the first time the term appears in an ESG DISCLOSURE STATEMENT.

Screening

References

Screening—General

"**Screening:** The application of filters to lists of potential securities, issuers, investments or sectors to rule investments in or out based on an investor's preferences, such as ethics and values, and/or investment metrics, such as risk assessments. Screening covers screening conducted under a manager's policy and client-directed screening."

—PRI, "Reporting Framework Glossary," 2021

Screening/Exclusion—Negative screening, ethical screening, faith-based screening

"**Ethical and faith-based investment:** Ethical (also known as values-driven) and faith-based investment refers to investing in line with certain principles, usually using negative screening to avoid investing in companies whose products and services are deemed morally objectionable by the investor or certain religions, international declarations, conventions or voluntary agreements."

—CFA Institute, "Certificate in ESG Investing: Official Training Manual," 3rd Edition, 2021

"**Negative screening/exclusions/negative exclusionary screens:** Excluding certain sectors, companies or projects for their poor ESG performance relative to industry peers or based on specific ESG criteria (e.g., avoiding particular products, services or business practices)."

—PRI, "Reporting Framework Glossary," 2021

"**Negative/exclusionary screening:** The exclusion from a fund or portfolio of certain sectors, companies, countries or other issuers based on activities considered not investable. Exclusion criteria (based on norms and values) can refer, for example, to product categories (e.g., weapons, tobacco), company practices (e.g., animal testing, violation of human rights, corruption) or controversies."

—GSIA, "Global Sustainable Investment Review 2020," 2020

Screening—Norms-based

"**Norms-based screening:** Screening investments against minimum standards of business practice based on international norms. Widely recognized frameworks for minimum standards of business practice include UN treaties, Security Council sanctions, UN Global Compact, Universal Declaration of Human Rights and OECD guidelines."

—PRI, "Reporting Framework Glossary," 2021

"**Norms-based screening:** Screening of investments against minimum standards of business or issuer practice based on international norms such as those issued by the UN, ILO [International Labour Organization], OECD and NGOs [non-governmental organizations] (e.g., Transparency International)."

—GSIA, "Global Sustainable Investment Review 2020," 2020

Screening—Positive screening, best-in-class screening

"**Best-in-class investment:** Best-in-class investment involves selecting only the companies that overcome a defined ranking hurdle, established using ESG criteria within each sector or industry."

—CFA Institute, "Certificate in ESG Investing: Official Training Manual," 3rd Edition, 2021

"**Positive/best-in-class screening:** Investing in sectors, companies or projects selected for their positive ESG performance relative to industry peers."

—PRI, "Reporting Framework Glossary," 2021

"**Best-in-class/positive screening**: Investment in sectors, companies or projects selected for positive ESG performance relative to industry peers, and that achieve a rating above a defined threshold."

—GSIA, "Global Sustainable Investment Review 2020," 2020

3.B.3 The INVESTMENT MANAGER SHOULD provide a definition for the term "screening" (including variants that refer to a specific type of screening) the first time the term appears in an ESG DISCLOSURE STATEMENT.

Thematic and Sustainability Themed Investing

References

"**Thematic investment:** Thematic investment refers to selecting companies that fall under a sustainability-related theme, such as clean-tech, sustainable agriculture, healthcare, or climate change mitigation."

—CFA Institute, "Certificate in ESG Investing: Official Training Manual," 3rd Edition, 2021

"**Thematic investing:** The identification and allocation of capital to themes or assets related to certain environmental or social outcomes, such as clean energy, energy efficiency, or sustainable agriculture."

—PRI, "Reporting Framework Glossary," 2021

"**Sustainability Themed/Thematic investing:** Investing in themes or assets specifically contributing to sustainable solutions—environmental and social (e.g., sustainable agriculture, green buildings, lower carbon tilted portfolio, gender equity, diversity)."

—GSIA, "Global Sustainable Investment Review 2020," 2020

"**Sustainable investment:** Sustainable investment refers to the selection of assets that contribute in some way to a sustainable economy, i.e., an asset that minimizes natural and social resource depletion. It is a broad term that may be used for the consideration of typical ESG issues and may include best-in-class. It can also include ESG integration, which considers how ESG issues impact a security's risk and return profile."

—CFA Institute, "Certificate in ESG Investing: Official Training Manual," 3rd Edition, 2021

3.B.4 The INVESTMENT MANAGER SHOULD provide a definition for the terms "thematic" and "sustainable" the first time they appear in an ESG DISCLOSURE STATEMENT.

Impact Investing

References

"**Impact Investing:** Impact investing refers to investments made with the specific intent of generating positive, measurable social and environmental impact alongside a financial return (which differentiates it from philanthropy)."

—CFA Institute, "Certificate in ESG Investing: Official Training Manual," 3rd Edition, 2021

"**Impact investments:** Impact investments are investments made with the intention to generate positive, measurable social and environmental impact alongside a financial return."

—Global Impact Investing Network,
"What You Need to Know about Impact Investing," 2021

"**Impact investing:** Investing to achieve positive, social and environmental impacts—requires measuring and reporting against these impacts, demonstrating the intentionality of investor and underlying asset/investee, and demonstrating the investor contribution."

—GSIA, "Global Sustainable Investment Review 2020," 2020

"**Community investing:** Where capital is specifically directed to traditionally underserved individuals or communities, as well as financing that is provided to businesses with a clear social or environmental purpose. Some community investing is impact investing, but community investing is broader and considers other forms of investing and targeted lending activities."

—GSIA, "Global Sustainable Investment Review 2020," 2020

3.B.5 The INVESTMENT MANAGER SHOULD use the term "impact investments" (and its variants) in a manner consistent with the previously referenced definitions.

3.B.6 The INVESTMENT MANAGER SHOULD provide a definition for the term "impact" (and its variants) and the term "impact investments" (and its variants) the first time either term appears in an ESG DISCLOSURE STATEMENT.

3.B.7 The INVESTMENT MANAGER SHOULD NOT describe an INVESTMENT PRODUCT as having a positive ENVIRONMENTAL or SOCIAL impact if there is not at least a significant allocation to "impact investments" as defined by the previously referenced definitions.

GLOSSARY

The definitions in this Glossary are specific to the Global ESG Disclosure Standards for Investment Products.

ENVIRONMENTAL	Relating to the quality and functioning of the natural environment and natural systems.
ESG	Abbreviation for "ENVIRONMENTAL, SOCIAL, GOVERNANCE, or some combination thereof."
ESG APPROACH	One of a variety of methods for incorporating ESG considerations into an INVESTMENT PRODUCT's objectives, investment process, or STEWARDSHIP ACTIVITIES. This term includes but is not limited to approaches that are often referred to as ESG integration, exclusion, screening, best-in-class, thematic, sustainability themed investing, impact investing, and stewardship.
ESG DISCLOSURE STATEMENT	A document that contains all of the disclosures REQUIRED by the Global ESG Disclosure Standards for Investment Products that apply to a specific INVESTMENT PRODUCT.
ESG INDEX	An index that includes ESG considerations in its index construction methodology.
ESG STANDARDS COMPLIANCE NOTIFICATION FORM	The form REQUIRED to be filed with CFA Institute by an INVESTMENT MANAGER to notify CFA Institute of the INVESTMENT MANAGER's use of the Global ESG Disclosure Standards for Investment Products.
GOVERNANCE	Relating to the policies and procedures used to direct, control, and monitor companies and other investee entities.
INTERPRETIVE GUIDANCE	Interpretive and explanatory materials related to the Global ESG Disclosure Standards for Investment Products issued by CFA Institute and the Global ESG Disclosure Standards for Investment Products' governing bodies, including but not limited to guidance statements, interpretations, and Q&As.
INVESTMENT MANAGER	An organization that manages an INVESTMENT PRODUCT.

INVESTMENT PRODUCT

A vehicle managed by an INVESTMENT MANAGER that uses INVESTORS' capital to buy, sell, and hold investments for the benefit of the INVESTOR, including but not limited to the following:

- An investment company, corporation, trust, or other vehicle that allows INVESTORS the ability to pool their capital and invest it collectively ("pooled funds")—such as open-end and closed-end mutual funds, unit investment trusts, exchange-traded funds (ETFs), Undertakings for the Collective Investment in Transferable Securities (UCITS), and Société d'investissement à Capital Variable (SICAV funds), as well as certain hedge funds, real estate funds, private equity funds, private debt funds, and pension funds.
- A contract between an INVESTOR and an INVESTMENT MANAGER—such as certain insurance-based INVESTMENT PRODUCTS and pension products.
- A limited partnership in which INVESTORS are limited partners and the INVESTMENT MANAGER is the general partner—such as certain hedge funds, real estate funds, and private equity funds.
- An investment strategy by which individually owned accounts are managed.

A vehicle offered by an INVESTMENT MANAGER that is wholly or partially sub-advised is considered an INVESTMENT PRODUCT of that INVESTMENT MANAGER, provided that the INVESTMENT MANAGER has discretion over the selection of the sub-advisor.

Note: The definition of INVESTMENT PRODUCT excludes certain types of financial products, including demand deposit accounts (e.g., checking and saving accounts), brokerage accounts in which clients direct their own trading activity, and all types of property and liability insurance.

INVESTOR

Any person or entity that currently invests in, or that has expressed interest and is qualified to invest in, an INVESTMENT PRODUCT.

Note: The definition of INVESTOR includes retail investors, wealth management clients, and institutional investors. Investment consultants and other third parties are considered to be INVESTORS if they represent individuals or entities that are INVESTORS.

MUST

A provision, task, or action that is mandatory or REQUIRED to be followed. (See "REQUIRE/REQUIREMENT.")

MUST NOT

A task or action that is forbidden or prohibited.

or

Note: Although not a defined term, the use of the word "or" is inclusive and means "X, or Y, or both" and "X, or Y, or Z, or some combination thereof." The use of "either…or" is exclusive and means "X or Y, but not both."

RECOMMEND/ RECOMMENDATION	A suggested provision, task, or action that SHOULD be followed or performed. A RECOMMENDATION is considered to be best practice but is not a REQUIREMENT. (See "SHOULD.")
REQUIRE/ REQUIREMENT	A provision, task, or action that MUST be followed or performed. (See "MUST".)
SHOULD	A provision, task, or action that is RECOMMENDED to be followed or performed and is considered to be best practice but is not REQUIRED.
SHOULD NOT	A task or action that is RECOMMENDED not to be followed or performed and is considered best practice not to do so.
SOCIAL	Relating to the rights, well-being, and interests of people, communities, and society.
STEWARDSHIP ACTIVITIES	Individual or collaborative activities, undertaken by an INVESTMENT MANAGER on behalf of INVESTORS, to protect and enhance the value of an INVESTMENT PRODUCT's holdings and to attain an INVESTMENT PRODUCT's objectives. STEWARDSHIP ACTIVITIES include but are not limited to engagement with issuers (in all asset classes and for both current and potential investees); voting at shareholder meetings; filing of shareholder resolutions/proposals; direct roles on investee boards and board committees; negotiation with and monitoring of the stewardship actions of suppliers in the investment chain; engagement with policymakers; engagement with standard setters; contributions to public goods (such as research) and public discourse (such as media) that support stewardship goals; and, where necessary, litigation.

APPENDIX A: DETERMINING THE APPLICABILITY OF PROVISIONS

This section provides examples for the purpose of illustrating the disclosure provisions that apply when specific ESG approaches are used in an investment product in a specific manner. These examples are provided as guidance. It is always the responsibility of the investment manager to determine the provisions that apply when preparing an ESG Disclosure Statement for a specific investment product.

It should not be assumed that:

- an example represents any specific investment product,
- the examples together represent an exhaustive list of all ESG approaches, or
- the examples represent mutually exclusive ESG approaches.

The examples provided are deliberately simple in nature and show only one ESG approach per example. In practice, many investment products use a combination of ESG approaches. In such instances, these examples can still be used as a guide. If an investment product, for example, uses the ESG approach illustrated in Example 1 along with the ESG approach illustrated in Example 3, then the applicable provisions for the investment product would be the combination of the applicable provisions shown in Example 1 and Example 3.

Example 1: "ESG Integration" is the Only ESG Approach Used in the Investment Product

Note: This is an illustrative example. It should not be assumed that the following list of characteristics constitutes a minimum set of requirements that an investment product must meet in order to be labeled, classified, or described using the term "ESG integration." Additionally, it should not be assumed that every investment product that is described or classified using the term "ESG integration" has these characteristics.

For this example, the following conditions are assumed:

- Financially material ESG information is systematically considered in investment decisions. ESG information is one type of information in a mosaic of financially material information, and the investment manager uses its discretion to determine how much weight to give ESG information in any particular investment decision.
- The investment manager uses the investment product's position of ownership to influence investees and issuers to disclose ESG information that the investment manager deems financially material.
- No other ESG approaches are used.

In this case, the following provisions apply: 1.A.1–1.A.10; 1.B.1; 2.A.1–2.A.3, 2.A.6, 2.A.7, 2.A.16, 2.A.18; 3.B.1, 3.B.2.

Additional provisions may apply if the investment product varies in any way from the foregoing description. It is always the investment manager's responsibility to determine the provisions that apply when preparing an ESG Disclosure Statement for a specific investment product.

Example 2: The Investment Product is Passively Managed to an Index Whose Construction Methodology Includes "Faith-based Screening," and No Other ESG Approaches are Used

Note: This is an illustrative example. It should not be assumed that the following list of characteristics constitutes a minimum set of requirements that an investment product must meet in order to be labeled, classified, or described using the term "faith-based screening." Additionally, it should not be assumed that every investment product that is described or classified using the term "faith-based screening" has these characteristics.

For this example, the following conditions are assumed:

- The investment product uses as an investment universe an ESG index that systematically excludes investments that conflict with certain faith-based principles.
- No other ESG approaches are used.

In this case, the following provisions apply: 1.A.1–1.A.10; 1.B.1; 2.A.1–2.A.4, 2.A.8, 2.A.16, 2.A.18; 3.B.3.

Additional provisions may apply if the investment product varies in any way from the foregoing description. It is always the investment manager's responsibility to determine the provisions that apply when preparing an ESG Disclosure Statement for a specific investment product.

Example 3: "Norms-based Screening" is the Only ESG Approach Used in the Investment Product

Note: This is an illustrative example. It should not be assumed that the following list of characteristics constitutes a minimum set of requirements that an investment product must meet in order to be labeled, classified, or described using the term "norms-based screening." Additionally, it should not be assumed that every investment product that is described or classified using the term "norms-based screening" has these characteristics.

For this example, the following conditions are assumed:

- The investment product has a policy to exclude from its portfolio the securities of any company that fails to abide by the United Nations Global Compact (UNGC) principles.
- The investment manager contracts with a third party to provide, on a regular basis, a list of companies that, based on in-depth research, fail to abide by the UNGC principles.
- The companies on the third-party list are flagged on the investment manager's trading system so that users are prevented from purchasing the securities of those companies.
- The companies that are on the third-party list are flagged on the investment manager's portfolio management system. If any of the companies' securities are held by the investment product, the portfolio management team is notified. Per policy, those securities are sold within 60 days.
- No other ESG approaches are used.

In this case, the following provisions apply: 1.A.1–1.A.10; 1.B.1; 2.A.1–2.A.4, 2.A.6, 2.A.9, 2.A.10, 2.A.16, 2.A.18; 3.B.3.

Additional provisions may apply if the investment product varies in any way from the foregoing description. It is always the investment manager's responsibility to determine the provisions that apply when preparing an ESG Disclosure Statement for a specific investment product.

Example 4: The Investment Product has a Focus on "Sustainable" Investments, and No Other ESG Approaches are Used

Note: This is an illustrative example. It should not be assumed that the following list of characteristics constitutes a minimum set of requirements that an investment product must meet in order to be labeled, classified, or described using the term "sustainable." Additionally, it should not be assumed that every investment product that is described or classified using the term "sustainable" has these characteristics.

For this example, the following conditions are assumed:

- The investment product has a policy that defines a sustainable investment to be any security of a company that has at least a 50% alignment with the EU Taxonomy based on turnover, as calculated per the methodology included in the Final Report of the Technical Expert Group on Sustainable Finance, March 2020.
- The investment manager has contracted with a third-party ESG data supplier to provide EU Taxonomy alignment data for companies in the investment product's investment universe.
- The investment product aims to allocate 70% of its funds to sustainable investments.

- Despite an intention to invest in sustainable economic activities, the investment product does not seek to attain specific environmental or social impact objectives.
- No other ESG approaches are used.

In this case, the following provisions apply: 1.A.1–1.A.10; 1.B.1; 2.A.1–2.A.4, 2.A.6, 2.A.14, 2.A.15, 2.A.16, 2.A.18; 3.B.4.

Additional provisions may apply if the investment product varies in any way from the foregoing description. It is always the investment manager's responsibility to determine the provisions that apply when preparing an ESG Disclosure Statement for a specific investment product.

Example 5: "Engagement" is the Only ESG Approach Used in the Investment Product

Note: This is an illustrative example. It should not be assumed that the following list of characteristics constitutes a minimum set of requirements that an investment product must meet in order to be labeled, classified, or described using the term "engagement." Additionally, it should not be assumed that every investment product that is described or classified using the term "engagement" has these characteristics.

For this example, the following conditions are assumed:

- The investment product is passively managed to a broad market equity index.
- The investment manager uses engagement to influence company management to improve the company's policies, practices, and behaviors related to ESG issues.
- No other ESG approaches are used.

In this case, the following provisions apply: 1.A.1–1.A.10; 1.B.1; 2.A.1–2.A.4, 2.A.16-2.A.18.

Additional provisions may apply if the investment product varies in any way from the foregoing description. It is always the investment manager's responsibility to determine the provisions that apply when preparing an ESG Disclosure Statement for a specific investment product.

APPENDIX B: SAMPLE ESG DISCLOSURE STATEMENTS

The samples below are illustrative examples of ESG Disclosure Statements. The purpose of these samples is to show how the provisions of the Standards can be met for a variety of investment products that use a variety of ESG approaches. The samples are not intended to provide "boilerplate" language for disclosures. Investment managers are responsible for the information they disclose in their ESG Disclosure Statements.

It should not be assumed that:

- a sample represents any specific investment product,
- any portion of any sample will satisfy a specific provision for a specific investment product, or
- disclosures that differ from the ones shown in the samples would not satisfy a specific provision for a specific investment product.

SAMPLE 1

XYZ Equity Strategy
ESG Disclosure Statement

This ESG Disclosure Statement for 1 January 2019 through 31 December 2021 complies with the disclosure requirements of the Global ESG Disclosure Standards for Investment Products. Additionally, XYZ Asset Management Company has complied with the requirements of the Global ESG Disclosure Standards for Investment Products related to the preparation and presentation of this ESG Disclosure Statement.

The Global ESG Disclosure Standards for Investment Products are developed and maintained by CFA Institute. CFA Institute does not endorse or promote this organization, nor does it warrant the accuracy or quality of the content contained herein.

Summary

The XYZ Equity Strategy (the "Strategy") uses ESG integration—the systematic and explicit inclusion of material environmental, social, and governance (ESG) data—in its pursuit of long-term capital growth. We consider financially material ESG data to be part of a comprehensive analysis of security risk and valuation. The XYZ Asset Management Company ("XYZ") ESG analysis and integration process applies to all equity securities; ESG data are not considered for the Strategy's money market securities.

The Strategy avoids certain types of investments that contribute in a negative manner to certain ESG issues. In addition, the Strategy excludes investments in companies that derive revenue from thermal coal mining and coal power generation because XYZ believes the coal industry is at significant economic risk as the world transitions to a lower carbon economy.[2]

XYZ considers ESG issues that are financially relevant to a company when voting proxies and engaging the management of that company.

Sources and Types of ESG Information

The Strategy uses ESG data to evaluate certain exclusion criteria, to analyze investments, and to inform proxy voting and engagement. ESG data is obtained primarily from two third-party ESG data providers, and additional information is obtained as needed through in-house analysis of company reports and regulatory filings as well as other sources, such as industry or nonprofit organizations. XYZ has conducted due diligence on the data collection and data governance processes of its ESG data providers. Because ESG data quality can be inconsistent, samples of the data from external sources are cross-referenced on a quarterly basis against company-disclosed data, other original source data, and between ESG data vendors. Acceptable data variance limits are determined per type of data by XYZ's data scientists. ESG data that exceed the variance limits are evaluated further by XYZ's sustainability analysts to determine which source of data will be used. Financially material ESG data for some companies may be unavailable or may fail to meet XYZ's data quality standards. In these cases, the weight of the company in the portfolio will not exceed 1% of the portfolio's market value, and the weight of all such companies in the portfolio will not exceed 10% of the portfolio's market value.

Screening Related to ESG Issues

XYZ applies exclusions to the Strategy's equity securities. Exclusions are not applied to the Strategy's money market securities. Exclusions are determined based on either industry codes or revenue thresholds. XYZ receives a monthly list from one of its ESG data providers of securities to be excluded from its portfolios based on the defined exclusion criteria. Exclusion criteria are applied at the onset of the security selection screening process. Securities that meet any of the criteria listed below are excluded from the security selection universe. If a current holding is subsequently found to be in violation of XYZ's exclusion criteria, the security will be sold within 60 days.

---

[2]The Strategy's investment policy was amended as of 1 January 2020 to exclude companies deriving revenues from thermal coal mining and coal power generation.

Tobacco

- Companies that have a Standard Industrial Classification (SIC) code in Major Group 21. This group includes businesses primarily engaged in manufacturing cigarettes, cigars, smoking and chewing tobacco, snuff, reconstituted tobacco, non-tobacco cigarettes, and in stemming and re-drying tobacco; or
- Companies that earned more than 5% of their annual revenue in their most recent fiscal year from the sale or distribution of cigarettes, cigars, smokeless and chewing tobacco, snuff, and non-tobacco cigarettes.

Alcohol

- Companies that have a Standard Industrial Classification (SIC) code of 2082 (Malt Beverages), 2084 (Wines, Brandy, and Brandy Spirits), or 2085 (Distilled and Blended Liquors); or
- Companies that earned more than 5% of their annual revenues from the sale or distribution of alcoholic beverages in their most recent fiscal year.

Pornography

- Companies that produce or distribute pornography. Zero tolerance revenue threshold.

Gambling

- Companies that earned more than 5% of their annual revenue in their most recent fiscal year from the offering of gambling.

Controversial Weapons

- Companies that produce, distribute, or maintain controversial weapons and key components thereof. Controversial weapons include but are not limited to cluster munitions; anti-personnel landmines; and biological, chemical, and nuclear weapons. The Strategy also complies with Regulation 123-4567, which requires the exclusion of cluster munitions and anti-personnel landmines.

Coal

- Companies that derive revenue from thermal coal mining or coal power generation. Zero tolerance revenue threshold.

Integration of ESG Data into Financial Analysis and Valuation

Identification of Material ESG Issues

In the XYZ investment process, we consider material ESG factors alongside traditional financial factors to provide a more comprehensive view of a security's long-term value and risk potential. Our team of data scientists gathers financial and ESG research and data from multiple sources, including company-issued reports and regulatory filings, industry associations, third-party investment research, market data, and ESG data providers. Our data scientists evaluate all ESG data used in the investment process. Data that is not verifiable or that cannot be reasonably estimated does not meet our data quality standards and is not used in our investment analysis process.

Our sector analysts are responsible for assessing material ESG factors for each industry they cover. They begin by referencing the Sustainability Accounting Standards Board (SASB) Standards. These standards are used to identify ESG metrics that are most likely to have a material financial effect on a company's operations based on the industry in which the company operates. Relevant environmental, social, and human capital issues are identified per industry, and our sector analysts consider industry-relevant SASB metrics for each company. This analysis is supplemented by an analysis of a company's unique characteristics, including its geographic location, which can introduce region-specific ESG risks such as climate-change-related risks.

Whereas the importance of certain environmental and social considerations varies greatly across industries, governance considerations remain fairly consistent. Material corporate governance issues evaluated for each company include board structure, independence, and composition; skill sets and level of experience of board directors and members; executive remuneration, and shareholder voting rights.

Finally, ESG data materiality is assessed based on the analyst's estimated investment horizon for an individual security. If an ESG factor is projected to have a negative short-term material effect on a company's valuation, the security may still be purchased or held if the analyst's investment horizon exceeds the projected short-term effect. Conversely, an ESG factor that is expected to have positive material benefits for a company over the long term will not be considered in the valuation of that security if the analyst's investment horizon for the security is short.

Integration of Material ESG Data

Quantitative and qualitative ESG data deemed material to a security's future financial performance are considered by XYZ's sector analysts alongside other material information when assessing historical company performance; making forward-looking estimates of earnings and revenues, operating and non-operating expenses, capital expenditures, and assets and liabilities; and comparing the company with its industry peers. Analysts also assess how well a company understands and manages the identified ESG risks. XYZ has developed a proprietary regression model to estimate the impact of a company's governance factors on its projected performance.

Our analysts may use the output from this model to raise or lower their estimated risk premium for a company.

Consideration of ESG Issues in Proxy Voting and Engagement

XYZ votes company proxies and engages company management for its equity holdings on a firm-wide basis solely in the best interests of our clients, in a manner intended to enhance the economic value of the securities held in the portfolio.

All proxy votes are recorded and stored in the XYZ proxy voting and engagement system. When the Proxy Voting Committee has voted against management on an issue, the engagement team initiates an engagement effort to discuss specific concerns with management via email. The XYZ engagement team also proactively engages with companies to encourage best governance practices, given that poor governance practices have been shown to impact company performance. Once an engagement effort has been initiated, a file is created in the proxy voting and engagement system that includes the company name, the specific issue identified, the targeted outcome, and a copy of the initial written communication. An automatic alert is put in place based on the recommended follow-up time frame. The XYZ engagement team tracks and reviews engagement efforts and progress on an ongoing basis. Continued engagement efforts are determined in accordance with the XYZ engagement policy. All written communications and summaries of meetings with company management are documented and maintained in the centralized internal database. The engagement team provides quarterly updates to portfolio managers and meets with them as needed.

Investors can obtain information about the Strategy's engagement activities and proxies voted and may request a copy of the Strategy's proxy voting and engagement policies and procedures by emailing clientsupport@xyzassetmanagement.com or writing to XYZ Asset Management Company, ATTN: Compliance Department, 1234 Alpha Summit Lane, Suite 1111, New York, NY 10005.

SAMPLE 2

ABC Growth and Income Fund
ESG Disclosure Statement

This ESG Disclosure Statement for 1 October 2019 through 31 March 2021 complies with the disclosure requirements of the Global ESG Disclosure Standards for Investment Products. Additionally, ABC Fund Management, Inc. has complied with the requirements of the Global ESG Disclosure Standards for Investment Products related to the preparation and presentation of this ESG Disclosure Statement.

The Global ESG Disclosure Standards for Investment Products are developed and maintained by CFA Institute. CFA Institute does not endorse or promote this organization, nor does it warrant the accuracy or quality of the content contained herein.

Summary

Sustainability is an important consideration for the ABC Growth and Income Fund (the "Fund"). ABC Fund Management defines sustainability as the "the responsible and efficient consumption and management of natural resources that allow future generations to meet their own needs." Some of the most important sustainability issues include the burning of fossil fuels and the resulting negative effect on global temperatures and climate. ABC Fund Management believes that the companies that use fossil fuels efficiently, implement energy-efficiency projects, or transition to renewable energy sources not only ensure their own continuity but also contribute to a more sustainable economy.

In consideration of these issues, the Fund seeks to achieve its investment objective through a broad market equity and fixed-income portfolio that has:

- at least a 50% lower weighted average carbon intensity (WACI) relative to the Fund's benchmark, and
- at least 25% of the market value of its fixed-income investments invested in labeled green bonds and Certified Climate Bonds.

Additionally, ABC Fund Management considers relevant climate change and natural resource management issues when voting proxies and engaging with company management.

Key ESG Terms

- *Carbon intensity* measures how efficiently a company uses its carbon resources to generate revenue and allows for comparison of carbon efficiency among companies of different sizes. Carbon intensity is calculated as a company's Scope 1 + Scope 2 greenhouse gas (GHG) emissions in carbon dioxide equivalents (CO_2e) normalized by USD1 million in revenue.
- *A carbon dioxide equivalent, or CO_2e,* is a measure used to compare the emissions from various greenhouse gases on the basis of their global-warming potential by converting amounts of other gases to the equivalent amount of carbon dioxide with the same global warming potential. (Source: Eurostat, based on a report from the European Environmental Agency)
- *Scope 1 emissions* are direct GHG emissions from sources owned or controlled by the company.
- *Scope 2 emissions* are indirect GHG emissions generated by the company's consumption of purchased electricity, heating, steam, and cooling.

- *Labeled green bonds* are bonds that earmark proceeds for climate or environmental projects and have been labeled as "green" by the issuer. (Source: Climate Bonds Initiative)
- *Certified Climate Bonds* are bonds and loans that are verified to conform with the Climate Bonds Standard, science-based standards for identifying projects and assets that are consistent with the Paris Agreement goals for a low-carbon economy. (Source: Climate Bonds Initiative)

Key ESG Data Used by the Fund

ABC Fund Management obtains carbon intensity data on companies in the Fund's universe from an ESG data provider. A company's Scope 1 and Scope 2 emissions and revenue are used to calculate its carbon intensity. Not all companies report their GHG emissions. If a company does not report its Scope 1 and Scope 2 emissions, the Fund's ESG data provider estimates the non-reported emissions using proprietary models. No universal method exists for estimating the GHG emissions of a company, and thus carbon intensity measures for individual companies can vary greatly among data providers. ABC Fund Management has chosen a data provider that obtains emissions data from multiple sources (including company-reported data, third party data, and its own proprietary estimates) and whose combined Scope 1 and Scope 2 company emissions estimates have been demonstrated to generally correlate well with those of other data providers.

Portfolio-Level ESG Characteristics and Allocation Target

Carbon Intensity Target

The weighted average carbon intensity of the Fund is the aggregate carbon intensity of the Fund's holdings according to the percentage weighting of each holding in the Fund. The WACI target is recalculated quarterly to reflect changes in the WACI of the benchmark indexes. To achieve the Fund's investment objective as well as its WACI target, the Fund invests in companies with attractive valuations and lower carbon intensity relative to industry peers. At times, the WACI target may not be attained because of natural variations in the carbon intensity of index constituents and changes made to index constituents. The Fund's WACI and WACI target are reported to investors in quarterly fund reports available on the Fund's website.

Target Allocation to Labeled Green Bonds and Climate Bonds

The Fund aims to invest at least 25% of the market value of its fixed-income holdings in labeled green bonds and Certified Climate Bonds. The Fund's allocation to labeled green bonds and Certified Climate Bonds is reported to investors in quarterly fund reports available on the Fund's website.

Proxy Voting and Engagement

The Fund's proxies are voted in accordance with the Fund's Proxy Voting Guidelines. Proxies are voted for all equity holdings of the Fund. Issues related to climate change and natural resource management are considered when voting on routine items, such as the election of directors, because ABC Fund Management believes prudent management of environmental issues can positively affect a company's financial performance and help mitigate climate change. Records of all proxy votes cast or abstained are maintained in our stewardship management system.

The Fund's Engagement Policy applies to its equity and fixed-income holdings. Engagement is undertaken with the intent to promote efforts to improve a company's carbon emissions and natural resource management. Engagement activities include in-person and virtual meetings, written correspondence, and emails. The Fund's engagement officer flags companies and issues for engagement. Once an engagement effort is initiated, all written communications and meeting records, including targeted outcomes of the engagement, are logged in the stewardship management system. Engagement may occur with a company's board of directors, executive management, or investor relations and may be conducted independently or in collaboration with other investors through the Fund's proxy voting and engagement service provider. On a quarterly basis, the Fund's engagement officer reviews progress made toward engagement goals relative to the targeted outcomes and determines next steps in accordance with the Engagement Policy.

The Proxy Voting Guidelines and Engagement Policy can be found on the Fund's website. ABC Fund Management also publishes an annual Proxy Voting and Engagement Report on the Fund's website that includes the past year's engagement priorities, progress on current engagements, and proxy voting activity.

SAMPLE 3

BCD Direct Investment Fund
ESG Disclosure Statement

This ESG Disclosure Statement for 1 November 2020 through 31 October 2021 complies with the disclosure requirements of the Global ESG Disclosure Standards for Investment Products. Additionally, BCD Investing Ltd. has complied with the requirements of the Global ESG Disclosure Standards for Investment Products related to the preparation and presentation of this ESG Disclosure Statement.

The Global ESG Disclosure Standards for Investment Products are developed and maintained by CFA Institute. CFA Institute does not endorse or promote this organization, nor does it warrant the accuracy or quality of the content contained herein.

Summary

The BCD Direct Investment Fund (the "Fund") was created to help prevent biodiversity loss in critical habitats and ecosystems in South America. Through its impact investments,[3] the Fund seeks to contribute to UN Sustainable Development Goal 15: *Protect, restore and promote sustainable use of terrestrial ecosystems, sustainably manage forests, combat desertification, and halt and reverse land degradation and halt biodiversity loss.* South America is home to some of the most diverse ecosystems on the planet and also some of the most endangered. These habitats promote economic stability and growth, contribute to sustainable food sources and income for area inhabitants, and combat climate change. Biodiversity loss occurs for a number of reasons, including extensive deforestation and exploitive land management practices. The Fund provides a vehicle for investors to address these environmental challenges while earning a return on investment.

The BCD Direct Investment Fund intends to invest the Fund's £125 million of committed capital in direct equity and debt in enterprises that provide solutions to protect and restore fragile ecosystems and habitats through sustainable forestry and land management practices. The Fund does not invest in companies that do not meet our Responsible Investing Policy. In addition to supplying capital, BCD Investing Ltd. ("BCD") seeks to determine or influence the formulation of company policies related to biodiversity preservation as well as the Fund's Responsible Investment Policy through appropriate governance structures.

The Fund is a Signatory to the Operating Principles for Impact Management.

Objectives

The Fund seeks to generate its target internal rate of return (IRR) and meet key performance indicators (KPIs) for the Fund's environmental objectives over the life of the Fund. The expected life of the Fund is 10 years. Through its investments, the Fund expects to benefit area inhabitants who depend on the health of these ecosystems for income as well as wildlife that rely on these ecosystems for survival. On a broader scale, preservation of South American biodiversity and forests has important implications for society at large, including but not limited to climate mitigation from the prevention of the release of greenhouse gas emissions, a reduction in food insecurity from the implementation of sustainable agricultural practices, and the preservation of a rich source of natural resources that have yielded important medicinal solutions.

The Fund uses the IRIS[4] metrics shown below to establish impact performance goals for investments and measure biodiversity impact outcomes. We believe sustainable forestry and

---

[3]"**Impact investments:** Impact investments are investments made with the intention to generate positive, measurable social and environmental impact alongside a financial return."

—Global Impact Investing Network, "What You Need to Know about Impact Investing," 2021 (https://thegiin.org/impact-investing/need-to-know/%23s2)

[4]Information on IRIS metrics can be found at https://iris.thegiin.org/

land management practices will be key drivers of value creation for the Fund's investments and that attainment of the impact performance goals below will help the Fund achieve its target IRR. Progress toward these outcomes is measured and evaluated annually. If an investee or financed project fails to achieve measurable progress, as determined by annual metrics established prior to investment, our Sustainability Team will consult with management to establish a plan of corrective action.

KPI	IRIS Metric	Impact Performance Goal
1	Forest Management Plan—OI2622	200,000 hectares sustainably managed
2	Land Directly Controlled: Sustainably Managed—OI6912	300,000 hectares sustainably managed

Investment Process

The Fund seeks to invest its capital in enterprises that provide sustainable solutions for forestry products, soft commodity production, and smallholder agricultural practices. As a supplier of capital to companies that may otherwise be unable to obtain funding, the Fund contributes to the mitigation of biodiversity loss in South America.

Prior to making an investment, BCD assesses potential investees or issuers first for the likelihood of achieving predetermined KPIs related to biodiversity loss mitigation and second for the ability to contribute to the achievement of the target IRR over the life of the Fund. To meet the Fund's impact objectives, it may be necessary at times for the Fund to prioritize investments with a greater potential for impact relative to financial performance. The Fund will engage in these trade-offs while striving to achieve an IRR within the stated target range. All potential investments are also assessed in accordance with our Responsible Investment Policy (see "Responsible Investment Policy" section), and no investments will be made in enterprises that violate this policy.

Risks to Achieving the Fund's Impact Objectives

Several risks may hinder the achievement of the Fund's impact objectives. There is a risk that one or more of the sustainable forest management or technological solutions used by enterprises in which the Fund invests may prove ineffective. The Fund may invest in start-up ventures; there is a risk that one or more new ventures may exhaust their supply of capital before one or more of the Fund's impact objectives are achieved. There is a risk that natural disasters may affect the output of certain investees. There is a risk that political interference may hinder the attainment of one or more impact objectives. There is a risk that the Fund may be unable to identify a sufficient number of enterprises and projects in which to invest in order to meet its impact objectives.

Responsible Investment Policy

Before an investment in an enterprise or project can be made, the BCD due diligence process ensures the investment conforms to our Responsible Investment Policy by avoiding investments in enterprises or projects that:

- violate the United Nations Global Compact principles,
- unlawfully infringe on the ownership or claimant rights of an indigenous people as set forth by the United Nations Declaration of Rights of Indigenous Peoples,
- violate sustainable agricultural and forest management processes as specified in contractual shareholder agreements and debt covenants.

Adherence to this Responsible Investment Policy is monitored as part of our quarterly review of portfolio holdings. We conduct ad hoc meetings with and visits to underlying companies and projects in order to assess and monitor the level and quality of impact being generated and the adherence to our Responsible Investment Policy. If, during our monitoring and review process, we identify negative impact concerns, as specified by our Responsible Investment Policy, our Sustainability Team will engage with management to identify solutions and take corrective actions. If such efforts prove unsuccessful, we will evaluate the feasibility of selling the enterprise or loan in the secondary market given the estimated value of the investment and the secondary market conditions.

Reporting

Financial information at the Fund level and investee level is reported quarterly, and progress on KPIs at the Fund level and investee level is reported annually. Investors may access all Fund reports through a secure client portal on our website 90 days past quarter end.

Stewardship

BCD uses its position as a contributor of capital to set impact objectives and promote adherence to the Fund's Responsible Investment Policy for its investee companies through appropriate governance structures. When taking a controlling stake in an investment, BCD will hold a majority of the seats on the board of governors to set company policy consistent with these goals. When making minority investments, BCD seeks to hold a seat on each company's board of directors in order to influence policy formation goals and Responsible Investment Policy actions as set forth in the shareholder agreement. When making direct loans, the Note Purchasing Agreement will contain covenants determining investee impact objectives and specific actions required and prohibited in accordance with the Fund's Responsible Investment Policy practices. For current investors in the Fund, the Fund's Stewardship Policy and annual reports describing stewardship activities can be accessed through the secure client portal. Prospective investors may request a copy of the Fund's Stewardship Policy by emailing BCDInvesting@BCDInvestingLtd.com.

SAMPLE 4

QRS Equity Fund
ESG Disclosure Statement

This ESG Disclosure Statement for 1 July 2020 through 30 June 2021 complies with the disclosure requirements of the Global ESG Disclosure Standards for Investment Products. Additionally, QRS Asset Management Co., Inc. has complied with the requirements of the Global ESG Disclosure Standards for Investment Products related to the preparation and presentation of this ESG Disclosure Statement.

The Global ESG Disclosure Standards for Investment Products are developed and maintained by CFA Institute. CFA Institute does not endorse or promote this organization, nor does it warrant the accuracy or quality of the content contained herein.

Fund Objectives

The objectives of the QRS Equity Fund (the "Fund") are to (1) achieve an equity market rate of return over a long-term investment horizon, and (2) actively engage with portfolio companies to encourage them to reduce their greenhouse gas (GHG) emissions to levels consistent with a 1.5 degree Celsius warming limit, by 2030, in alignment with targets set by the Paris Agreement. Through its impact investing[5] efforts to achieve a measurable reduction in portfolio company GHG emissions, the Fund aims to contribute to the achievement of the United Nations Sustainable Development Goal 13, Climate Action: *Take urgent action to combat climate change and its impacts.*

Summary

Global warming affects many aspects of life on the planet, including human life, life on land, and life below water. In order to meet the Paris Agreement goals, global GHG emissions must be reduced to 50% of 2005 emissions by 2030 and to net zero emissions by 2050. The Fund aims to contribute to the mitigation of global warming by investing in companies with GHG emissions that exceed limits consistent with the Paris Agreement and using active engagement to bring about a reduction in company emissions in line with a 1.5 Celsius degree warming scenario. GHG emissions reduction targets and engagement goals for each of the Fund's portfolio companies are determined prior to investment.

[5]"**Impact Investing:** Impact investing refers to investments made with the specific intent of generating positive, measurable social and environmental impact alongside a financial return (which differentiates it from philanthropy)."

—CFA Institute, "Certificate in ESG Investing: Official Training Manual," 3rd Edition, 2021

Climate Data Sources and Limitations

We use external vendors and non-profit organizations to supply Scope 1 (direct) and Scope 2 (indirect) emissions,[6] either company-reported or vendor-estimated, for companies in the Fund's universe, as well as carbon intensity for each company. Carbon intensity is defined as the company's most recent reported or estimated Scope 1 + Scope 2 greenhouse gas emissions[7] in carbon dioxide equivalents[8] (CO_2e) normalized by USD1 million in revenue (metric tons of CO_2e per USD1 million in sales). Carbon intensity measures a company's energy efficiency.

Because company GHG emissions data are not standardized (and further subject to estimation error when not company-reported), the data sets we work with may imperfectly represent companies' true GHG emissions. Additionally, the company emissions targets that we set are based on model assumptions and estimations that carry the inherent risk associated with any modeling or estimating process.

Impact Strategy

Security selection begins with ranking companies in the Fund's universe within their industries according to their carbon intensity and analyzing the feasibility of using engagement to facilitate a meaningful reduction in GHG emissions. Financial analysis screens are applied to arrive at a set of securities that have the potential to meet both the Fund's financial and impact objectives. The Fund typically limits holdings to between 30 and 50 companies to provide for ongoing active and meaningful engagement with each company.

The Fund's sustainability analysts use a combination of data from third-party providers, non-profit organizations, and internal research to set individual, science-based, forward-looking GHG emissions targets for each investee. Both interim and long-term engagement goals may be set for a company, including but not limited to the following:

- Begin reporting on Scope 1 and Scope 2 emissions
- Achieve a target GHG emissions level
- Achieve a target carbon intensity measure
- Link executive compensation to achievement of the GHG emissions goal

Securities may be sold from the Fund if it is determined to be unlikely that a GHG emissions target for a company will be achieved or if it is believed that the company is no longer able to contribute to the Fund's financial objective. It may be necessary at times to invest in securities that

[6]Scope 1 emissions are direct GHG emissions from sources owned or controlled by the company. Scope 2 emissions are indirect GHG emissions arising from the use of purchased energy.

[7]The primary sources of GHGs are carbon dioxide (CO_2), methane (CH_4), and nitrous oxide (N_2O).

[8]A carbon dioxide equivalent, or CO_2e, refers to the number of metric tons of CO_2 emissions with the same global warming potential as one metric ton of another greenhouse gas.

will help the Fund meet its financial objective but that may not meet the Fund's impact objective. These securities will be limited to 20% or less of the Fund's market value.

The Fund's Sustainability Team monitors investee's impacts on biodiversity, water, waste, and human rights to ensure GHG emissions targets are not attained through a negative impact on other key ESG issues. There is a risk that a company in which the Fund invests subsequently generates an adverse social or environmental impact or event. In these instances, the Fund's Sustainability Team, in conjunction with the Fund's portfolio managers, determines whether to sell the security or whether to engage with the company in an attempt to mitigate the adverse consequences.

There is a risk that engagement efforts will not achieve the engagement goals set for a company. A company may choose not to respond to engagement efforts, or the company may experience a change in economic circumstances or a change in management that affects its ability or willingness to address GHG emissions reductions. In addition, there is a risk that an error was made in our emissions target and that the GHG emissions goal for a company or companies is not feasible.

Stewardship

Proxies are voted and engagement efforts are undertaken for all portfolio companies. Proxy voting may support either the Fund's financial objective or its impact objective. When voting in support of the Fund's impact objective, certain environmental and social issues are prioritized, including issues relating to climate change mitigation efforts, transparency in reporting of environmental and social metrics, and linking executive pay to certain ESG metrics.

Engagement is conducted in the form of written communications, collaborative engagement, and one-to-one meetings with representatives from a company's board of directors and management, investor relations, or sustainability team. By engaging with a company's board of directors or management to achieve a targeted reduction in reported GHG emissions, the Fund aims to have positive, measurable real-world outcomes that contribute to the Paris Agreement goals.

Engagement goals and GHG emissions targets for each portfolio company are logged into our stewardship engagement system, and engagement activities are tracked throughout the life of the holding. Achievement of engagement goals and GHG emissions targets is typically expected to be attained over a period of several years. Progress toward an emissions target may be measured through the achievement of interim goals or by the measurement of GHG emissions on a glidepath toward a targeted emissions level. Information about GHG emissions levels and carbon intensity for all holdings can be found in quarterly reports on the Fund's website.

The QRS Stewardship Team meets quarterly to review company progress and engagement responses. For some companies, engagement begins with the intent to achieve a short-term goal, such as the initiation of reporting Scope 1 and 2 emissions or to educate management on pathways to achieve a reduction in GHG emissions in order to obtain a later commitment to reduce GHG emissions. For other companies, a significant reduction in GHG emissions is the only impact metric. If the Stewardship Team determines that a company is not making sufficient progress toward a target or goal, engagement is escalated according to the Fund's Engagement Policy.

The Fund's Proxy Voting Policy and Guidelines, Engagement Policy, and Annual Engagement Impact Reports are available to investors on the Fund's website. Annual Engagement Impact Reports contain information on companies engaged with during the previous calendar year and the method of engagement, issues engaged on, progress toward GHG emissions targets and engagement goals, outlook for future engagement efforts, and tons of GHG emissions avoided per USD100 million at the Fund level. Investors may obtain information on proxies voted by writing to proxyvoting@QRSAssetManagement.com.

APPENDIX C: DEVELOPMENT OF THE GLOBAL ESG DISCLOSURE STANDARDS FOR INVESTMENT PRODUCTS

CFA Institute began exploring the need for ESG standards in 2019. Preliminary research indicated a need for standards in the areas of investment product disclosure and classification related to ESG approaches.

In January 2020, CFA Institute formed a volunteer ESG Working Group to explore concepts for voluntary global standards. The application process was open to anyone with the required level of ESG and investment industry experience. Volunteers were not required to be CFA charterholders or members of CFA Institute. Members were selected such that the group consisted of ESG experts from around the world and from various types of organizations, including asset owners, investment managers, consultants, service providers, and not-for-profit organizations. The ESG Working Group's efforts led to the August 2020 publication of the Consultation Paper on the Development of the CFA Institute ESG Disclosure Standards for Investment Products.[9] The Consultation Paper solicited feedback on the concepts proposed by the ESG Working Group. The ESG Working Group's planned one-year term ended in January 2021.

In November 2020, CFA Institute formed two new volunteer bodies, the ESG Technical Committee and the ESG Verification Subcommittee. These standing bodies have been, and will continue to be, responsible for guiding the development of the Standards. The ESG Technical Committee is responsible for guiding the development of the Standards' provisions—that is, its requirements and recommendations. The ESG Verification Subcommittee is responsible for guiding the development of the Standards' assurance procedures. As with the ESG Working Group, the application process was open to anyone with the required level of ESG and investment industry experience, and members were selected for expertise and a diversity of perspectives. The ESG Technical Committee's efforts led to the May 2021 publication of the Exposure Draft of the CFA Institute ESG Disclosure Standards for Investment Products.[10] The Exposure Draft solicited

[9]The Consultation Paper on the Development of the CFA Institute ESG Disclosure Standards for Investment Products represents the overall views of CFA Institute and the ESG Working Group. Although it represents such a consensus, it may not necessarily, with respect to all details, represent the individual views of Working Group members or their employers.

[10]The Exposure Draft of the CFA Institute ESG Disclosure Standards for Investment Products represents the overall views of CFA Institute and the ESG Technical Committee. Although it represents such a consensus, it may not necessarily, with respect to all details, reflect the individual views of ESG Technical Committee members or their employers.

feedback on a draft version of the Standards. The ESG Verification Subcommittee's efforts led to the July 2021 publication of the Exposure Draft of the Verification Procedures of the CFA Institute ESG Disclosure Standards for Investment Products,[11] which solicited feedback on a draft version of the assurance procedures.

[11]The Exposure Draft of the Verification Procedures for the CFA Institute ESG Disclosure Standards for Investment Products represents the overall views of CFA Institute and the ESG Verification Subcommittee. Although it represents such a consensus, it may not necessarily, with respect to all details, reflect the individual views of ESG Technical Committee members or their employers.

APPENDIX D: RELATIONSHIP TO REGULATIONS AND OTHER CODES AND STANDARDS

During the development of the Standards, CFA Institute staff reviewed approximately 125 regulations, principles, codes, standards, guides, reports, white papers, methodologies, classifications, labels, assessment tools, and questionnaires. The following regulations, frameworks, codes, and standards are the most relevant to the Standards insofar that the Standards have been designed to be complementary to them to the extent such was deemed feasible and practical given the purpose and scope of the Standards.

European Union (EU) Sustainable Finance Disclosure Regulation (SFDR)

Both the Standards and SFDR aim to foster transparency in investment product disclosures. Because SFDR is part of the EU's action plan for financing sustainable growth, SFDR also has the goals of reorienting capital flows towards sustainable investment, mainstreaming sustainability into risk management, and fostering long-termism in financial and economic activity. The Standards do not have these additional goals.

Because SFDR focuses on sustainability, it has more requirements than the Standards for the disclosure of sustainability-related information. Because the Standards aim to address all investment products that incorporate one or more ESG approaches, they can be applied to investment products that are not necessarily promoted as "sustainable"—for example, faith-based investment products and some impact investment products.

Regarding the scope of disclosures, three key differences exist between SFDR and the Standards. First, SFDR requires both entity-level disclosures and product-level disclosures, whereas the Standards require only product-level disclosures. Second, SFDR has disclosure requirements related to an investment product's ESG approaches and periodic reporting; the Standards cover only an investment product's ESG approaches. Third, SFDR has distinct disclosure requirements for regulatory documents and for websites; the Standards require only one set of disclosures, which can be provided to investors in multiple ways.

Other Investment Product ESG Disclosure Codes and Standards

There are three voluntary frameworks[12] that focus on transparency and comparability for certain types of investment products—the European SRI Transparency Code (for European retail funds), the Operating Principles for Impact Management (for impact strategies), and the INREV

[12]As of 1 November 2021.

Sustainability Reporting Guidelines (for non-listed real estate strategies). These three efforts address a number of important disclosure topics, many of which the Standards address as well. Those who are familiar with these frameworks will recognize their positive influence on the development of the Standards. Yet even when combined, these three frameworks do not cover all types of investment products and all regions. The Global ESG Disclosure Standards for Investment Products address both fragmentation (i.e., multiple standards that address only certain parts of the global investment product market) and gaps (i.e., those markets and types of investment products for which no standards exist) in the current state of ESG disclosures.

CFA Institute Codes and Standards

The Standards are consistent with the CFA Institute Code of Ethics and Standards of Professional Conduct. All members of CFA Institute (including CFA charterholders and CIPM certificants), as well as candidates for the CFA designation and the CIPM certificate, must adhere to the CFA Institute Code of Ethics and Standards of Professional Conduct. The CFA Institute Code of Ethics and Standards of Professional Conduct state, in part, that members and candidates must do the following:

- Disclose to clients and prospective clients the basic format and general principles of the investment processes they use to analyze investments, select securities, and construct portfolios and promptly disclose any changes that might materially affect those processes. (V.B.1)
- Disclose to clients and prospective clients significant limitations and risks associated with the investment process. (V.B.2)
- Use reasonable judgment in identifying which factors are important to their investment analyses, recommendations, or actions, and include those factors in communications with clients and prospective clients. (V.B.3)
- Distinguish between fact and opinion in the presentation of investment analysis and recommendations. (V.B.4)

Although the Global ESG Disclosure Standards for Investment Products are consistent with the CFA Institute Code of Ethics and Standards of Professional Conduct, this fact does not imply that members of CFA Institute, CFA charterholders, CIPM certificants, and candidates for the CFA designation and the CIPM certificate must comply with the Global ESG Disclosure Standards for Investment Products. (In fact, individuals cannot claim an ESG Disclosure Statement complies with the Global ESG Disclosure Standards for Investment Products—only investment management organizations can claim an ESG Disclosure Statement complies with the Global ESG Disclosure Standards for Investment Products.) Members of CFA Institute, CFA charterholders, CIPM certificants, and candidates for the CFA designation and the CIPM certificate will not be held accountable or penalized by CFA Institute if the organization that they work for or own does not prepare and make available ESG Disclosure Statements in compliance with the Global ESG Disclosure Standards for Investment Products.

The Standards are also consistent with the CFA Institute Asset Manager Code, a voluntary principles-based code that outlines a firm's ethical and professional responsibilities to clients. The CFA Institute Asset Manager Code states, in part, that investment managers must do the following:

- Ensure that disclosures are truthful, accurate, complete, and understandable and are presented in a format that communicates the information effectively. (F.1)
- Disclose the investment process, including information regarding lock-up periods, strategies, risk factors, and use of derivatives and leverage. (F.4.c)
- Disclose valuation methods used to make investment decisions and value client holdings. (F.4.g)
- Disclose shareholder voting policies. (F.4.h)

Although the Global ESG Disclosure Standards for Investment Products are consistent with the CFA Institute Asset Manager Code, this fact does not imply that asset managers who claim compliance with the Asset Manager Code must comply with the Global ESG Disclosure Standards for Investment Products, or vice versa. However, the Global ESG Disclosure Standards for Investment Products do offer detailed guidance about how to fulfill Asset Manager Code requirements when an investment product uses one or more ESG approaches.

ERRATA FOR THE GLOBAL ESG DISCLOSURE STANDARDS FOR INVESTMENT PRODUCTS

The following underlined items reflect added language to correct the Global ESG Disclosure Standards for Investment Products. Updated errata will be published on the ESG Disclosure Standards webpage hosted by CFA Institute.

Provision 1.A.2

The INVESTMENT MANAGER MUST comply with all REQUIREMENTS of the Global ESG Disclosure Standards for Investment Products, including any INTERPRETIVE GUIDANCE, that apply to <u>the INVESTMENT MANAGER as well as</u> a specific INVESTMENT PRODUCT in order to state that the ESG DISCLOSURE STATEMENT for that specific INVESTMENT PRODUCT has been prepared and presented in compliance with the Global ESG Disclosure Standards for Investment Products.

Provision 2.A.9

If an INVESTMENT PRODUCT has <u>ESG</u> criteria that systematically exclude certain investments OR has ESG criteria that need to be met in order for an investment to be considered for inclusion in the portfolio, then the INVESTMENT MANAGER MUST disclose for each <u>ESG</u> criterion:

a. the characteristic of the investment that is evaluated;

b. the threshold or condition against which the characteristic is compared;

c. whether the investment is excluded from, or is eligible for inclusion in, the portfolio when the threshold or condition is met; and

d. a reference, where applicable, to any law, regulation, or third-party standard, guideline, or framework used in the establishment or evaluation of the <u>ESG</u> criterion.

Provision 2.A.10

If an INVESTMENT PRODUCT has ESG criteria that systematically exclude certain investments or has ESG criteria that need to be met in order for an investment to be considered for inclusion in the portfolio, then the INVESTMENT MANAGER MUST disclose:

a. where the ESG criteria are applied in the investment process.

b. the exceptions to the application of the ESG criteria, if any.

 |

EXPLANATION OF THE PROVISIONS OF THE GLOBAL ESG DISCLOSURE STANDARDS FOR INVESTMENT PRODUCTS

INTRODUCTION

The Global ESG Disclosure Standards for Investment Products (the "ESG Disclosure Standards") are divided into three sections, which are as follows:

1: Fundamentals of Compliance

2: Investment Product ESG Disclosures

3: ESG Terminology

Section 1: Fundamentals of Compliance. The Fundamentals of Compliance section contains requirements pertaining to preparing ESG Disclosure Statements, ensuring that information presented is not false or misleading, adhering to all applicable laws and regulations, and making ESG Disclosure Statements available to investors.

Section 2: Investment Product ESG Disclosures. The Investment Product ESG Disclosures section contains requirements for disclosing information related to how an investment product considers ESG issues in its objectives, investment process, and stewardship activities.

Section 3: ESG Terminology. The ESG Terminology section contains recommendations for using ESG terminology in ESG Disclosure Statements.

The Explanation of the Provisions in Sections 1–3 provides interpretation of each provision contained in Sections 1–3. Each provision in each section is included in a grey text box. Within the provisions are words appearing in small capital letters that indicate defined terms. These defined terms can be found in the Glossary within the ESG Disclosure Standards. Following each provision is a discussion that provides interpretive guidance to help readers understand the provision.

1. FUNDAMENTALS OF COMPLIANCE

A. Fundamentals of Compliance–Requirements

Provision 1.A.1

The INVESTMENT MANAGER MUST comply with any laws and regulations that apply to the preparation and distribution of an ESG DISCLOSURE STATEMENT.

Discussion

The Global ESG Disclosure Standards for Investment Products (the "ESG Disclosure Standards") define an ESG Disclosure Statement as a document that contains all of the disclosures required by the Global ESG Disclosure Standards for Investment Products that apply to a specific investment product. Investment managers must comply with all applicable laws and regulations regarding the preparation and distribution of an ESG Disclosure Statement in the country or countries in which they are domiciled as well as those countries in which they do business. Compliance with applicable laws and regulations does not necessarily result in compliance with the ESG Disclosure Standards. Investment managers claiming compliance with the ESG Disclosure Standards must comply with all of the applicable requirements of the ESG Disclosure Standards in addition to all applicable laws and regulations.

If a disclosure required by the ESG Disclosure Standards is prohibited by law or regulation, an investment manager can still claim compliance with the ESG Disclosure Standards. In such instances, Provision 2.A.2 requires that the investment manager include a description of the prohibited disclosure requirement in the ESG Disclosure Statement along with an explanation of why the required disclosure cannot be included.

Provision 1.A.2

The INVESTMENT MANAGER MUST comply with all REQUIREMENTS of the Global ESG Disclosure Standards for Investment Products, including any INTERPRETIVE GUIDANCE, that apply to the INVESTMENT MANAGER as well as a specific INVESTMENT PRODUCT in order to state that the ESG DISCLOSURE STATEMENT for that specific INVESTMENT PRODUCT has been prepared and presented in compliance with the Global ESG Disclosure Standards for Investment Products.[1]

Discussion

Investment managers must comply with all requirements of the ESG Disclosure Standards that apply to the investment manager as well as to an ESG Disclosure Statement that has been prepared for a specific investment product. Requirements can be found within the provisions of the ESG Disclosure Standards and within interpretive guidance, which includes updates and clarifications issued by CFA Institute and the ESG Disclosure Standards governing bodies. Investment managers must review all of the requirements of the ESG Disclosure Standards to determine each requirement's applicability to the investment manager as well as to the ESG Disclosure Statement that has been prepared for a specific investment product.

Provision 1.A.3

An INVESTMENT MANAGER MUST NOT represent or state that an ESG DISCLOSURE STATEMENT is "in compliance with the Global ESG Disclosure Standards for Investment Products except for..." or make any other statements that may indicate partial compliance with the Global ESG Disclosure Standards for Investment Products.

Discussion

When an investment manager claims that an ESG Disclosure Statement complies with the Global ESG Disclosure Standards for Investment Products, the investment manager is representing that all of the applicable requirements of the ESG Disclosure Standards have been met for that ESG Disclosure Statement. The investment manager must not choose to comply with only selected applicable requirements. If an ESG Disclosure Statement for a particular investment product does not meet all of the applicable requirements of the ESG Disclosure Standards, the investment

[1] The Global ESG Disclosure Standards for Investment Products incorrectly omitted the words "the investment manager as well as" from Provision 1.A.2. Provision 1.A.2 as stated here is correct.

manager must not make any statements that indicate compliance or partial compliance with the ESG Disclosure Standards for that ESG Disclosure Statement.

Provision 1.A.4

The INVESTMENT MANAGER MUST NOT, in an ESG DISCLOSURE STATEMENT:

a. present information that is false or misleading.

Discussion

Investment managers must not present any information in an ESG Disclosure Statement that is known to be inaccurate or that may mislead investors. Disclosures must not misrepresent or overstate either the effect of an investment product's ESG approaches on ESG issues or the effect of ESG information on any aspect of an investment product.

Information that has a high risk of being false or misleading includes claims about the following:

- the positive effect or impact that an investment product has, or is expected to have, on one or more ESG issues;
- the investment product's contribution, or expected contribution, toward the advancement of third-party sustainable development goals;
- the use of ESG information in the investment process or in stewardship activities; and
- the effect of the investment product's exclusions on the investment product's investment process or consideration of ESG issues.

An ESG Disclosure Statement may include information beyond the information that is required by the ESG Disclosure Standards if the investment manager believes such information would help an investor to understand and evaluate the investment product. The inclusion of such information must not cause the ESG Disclosure Statement to be false or misleading.

Provision 1.A.4

The INVESTMENT MANAGER MUST NOT, in an ESG DISCLOSURE STATEMENT:

b. omit significant information about the INVESTMENT PRODUCT'S ESG APPROACHES.

Discussion

Complying with Provision 1.A.4.b may require the disclosure of more information than is explicitly required by the ESG Disclosure Standards. If the requirements of the ESG Disclosure Standards do not fully address a particular ESG approach or contain a requirement that is open to interpretation, the investment manager must disclose all significant information beyond the information that is required and recommended by the ESG Disclosure Standards. Significant information includes information that is relevant to a particular investment product and is important in helping an investor understand how the investment product considers ESG issues in its objectives, investment process, or stewardship activities.

Provision 1.A.4

The INVESTMENT MANAGER MUST NOT, in an ESG DISCLOSURE STATEMENT:

c. contradict disclosures made in the INVESTMENT PRODUCT's regulatory documents.

Discussion

The ESG Disclosure Standards may require the disclosure of information that is similar to information in disclosures or filings required by law or regulation. When this is the case, an investment manager is not required to include in the ESG Disclosure Statement the same language used in regulatory documents. The investment manager must ensure, however, that the information disclosed in the ESG Disclosure Statement is consistent with, and does not contradict, the information contained in regulatory documents.

Provision 1.A.5

The ESG DISCLOSURE STATEMENT MUST cover a minimum period of one year, or the period since inception if the INVESTMENT PRODUCT has existed for less than one year.

Discussion

An ESG Disclosure Statement must cover a minimum period of one year or, if the investment product has existed for less than one year, the period since the investment product's inception. The investment product inception date is the date on which the investment product's track record begins. As long as this requirement regarding the minimum period covered by an ESG Disclosure Statement is met, an investment manager is free to choose the period covered by an investment product's ESG Disclosure Statement. The period covered by an ESG Disclosure Statement must be included in the compliance statement required by Provision 2.A.1.g.

Investment managers do not need to wait one year after adding one or more ESG approaches to an investment product that previously included no ESG approaches to prepare an ESG Disclosure Statement. If one or more ESG approaches are added to an investment product that previously included no ESG approaches, and the addition of the ESG approaches occurred within the prior 12 months, the investment manager is still permitted to prepare an ESG Disclosure Statement for the investment product as long as the investment manager discloses the addition of the ESG approaches and the effective dates of the additions.

If an ESG Disclosure Statement covers a period during which a disclosed ESG approach is no longer included in an investment product, the information in the ESG Disclosure Statement would be considered false and misleading if the ESG Disclosure Statement is not updated to reflect the fact that the ESG approach is no longer in place.

Provision 1.A.6

The INVESTMENT MANAGER MUST document its policies and procedures for:

a. establishing and maintaining compliance with the REQUIREMENTS of the Global ESG Disclosure Standards for Investment Products, as well as any RECOMMENDATIONS it has chosen to adopt; and

b. monitoring and identifying changes and additions to the Global ESG Disclosure Standards for Investment Products and INTERPRETIVE GUIDANCE.

Discussion

Policies and procedures provide the investment manager with a sufficiently objective, relevant, and complete roadmap to making the disclosures required by the ESG Disclosure Standards as well as any adopted recommendations of the ESG Disclosure Standards. Documenting policies and procedures is essential to ensuring the validity of an investment manager's claim that an ESG Disclosure Statement for an investment product complies with the ESG Disclosure Standards. Investment managers must actively make a determination about the applicability of all the requirements of the ESG Disclosure Standards and document the relevant policies and procedures accordingly. Investment managers are not required, however, to create and document policies and procedures to comply with requirements that do not apply to the investment manager or the preparation of its ESG Disclosure Statements.

Once an investment manager establishes its policies and procedures, it must apply them consistently. Policies and procedures should be reviewed regularly to determine if they should be changed or improved, but it is not expected that they will change frequently. Investment managers must also create policies and procedures to monitor and identify changes and additions to the ESG Disclosure Standards and all of the interpretive guidance, which includes updates and clarifications issued by CFA Institute and the ESG Disclosure Standards governing bodies.

Investment managers should establish clear accountability for their compliance with the ESG Disclosure Standards. An investment manager should assign at least one person internally who is responsible for monitoring compliance with the ESG Disclosure Standards. Depending on the investment manager's size and complexity, maintaining compliance may require coordination across multiple departments, including but not limited to portfolio management, compliance, and marketing.

Provision 1.A.7

The INVESTMENT MANAGER MUST capture and maintain documents and records necessary to support the information included in an ESG DISCLOSURE STATEMENT.

Discussion

An investment manager must be able to substantiate its claim that an investment product's ESG Disclosure Statement complies with the ESG Disclosure Standards. It is important for investors, regulators, and assurance providers to have confidence that all information included in an ESG Disclosure Statement is supported by the appropriate documents and records.

There is no precise list of documents and records that must be maintained to support the information disclosed in an ESG Disclosure Statement. Each investment manager must determine for itself which documents and records must be maintained based on the disclosures it makes in an ESG Disclosure Statement. The actual documents and records required will depend on an investment manager's particular circumstances and may include the following:

- regulatory filings,
- investment policy statements,
- internal research and reports,
- vendor research and reports,
- documentation supporting investment decisions,
- records of stewardship activities,
- portfolio holdings,
- investor reports,

- marketing materials, and
- support for investment product labels or certifications.

In certain instances, the required documents and records may not be immediately available. For example, the investment manager may need to retrieve them from an offsite location or from a third-party service provider. However, the documents and records required to be maintained by this provision must be available in a usable format within a reasonable time frame. In all instances, either paper (hard copy) records or electronically stored records will suffice. If records are stored electronically, they must be accessible and able to be printed or downloaded, if needed. Documents and records stored in a system that is not operable and from which they cannot be retrieved will not satisfy the recordkeeping requirements.

Provision 1.A.8

The INVESTMENT MANAGER MUST notify CFA Institute of its use of the Global ESG Disclosure Standards for Investment Products by submitting the ESG STANDARDS COMPLIANCE NOTIFICATION FORM. This form MUST be filed:

a. when the INVESTMENT MANAGER initially completes an ESG DISCLOSURE STATEMENT for any one of its INVESTMENT PRODUCTS; and
b. thereafter annually between 1 January and 30 June.

Discussion

After an investment manager prepares its first ESG Disclosure Statement, the investment manager must submit the ESG Standards Compliance Notification Form to CFA Institute. The investment manager must not make any ESG Disclosure Statement available to investors until it has submitted the ESG Standards Compliance Notification Form to CFA Institute and has received an acknowledgement of submission from CFA Institute.

Once an investment manager has submitted its initial ESG Standards Compliance Notification Form, the investment manager is not required to submit an ESG Compliance Notification Form for any additional ESG Disclosure Statements that it prepares. Instead, the ESG Standards Compliance Notification Form must be updated annually between 1 January and 30 June. The period of any assurance engagement performed by an independent third party does not affect the submission date of the ESG Standards Compliance Notification Form.

Provision 1.A.9

If the INVESTMENT MANAGER chooses to apply the Global ESG Disclosure Standards for Investment Products to a specific INVESTMENT PRODUCT, the INVESTMENT MANAGER MUST make the ESG DISCLOSURE STATEMENT for that specific INVESTMENT PRODUCT available to INVESTORS.

Discussion

Investment managers that have prepared an ESG Disclosure Statement for an investment product must make the ESG Disclosure Statement available to investors. The ESG Disclosure Standards define an investor as any person or entity that currently invests in, or that has expressed interest and is qualified to invest in, an investment product. The definition of investor includes retail investors, wealth management clients, and institutional investors. Investment consultants, advisors, and other third parties are considered to be investors if they represent individuals or entities that are investors.

For some types of investment products, a qualified investor may be determined by local laws or regulations. For other types of investment products, an investment manager may establish its own criteria for determining who is qualified to invest in the investment product. For example, if the investment product is an institutional strategy available only to investors who meet certain criteria, the investment manager may establish a process to ensure investors meet those criteria prior to making the ESG Disclosure Statement available to them. In this case, an investment manager might require investors to fill out a form online in order to access the ESG Disclosure Statement.

It is the investment manager's obligation to make the ESG Disclosure Statement available to investors; an investment manager must not place the burden of obtaining an ESG Disclosure Statement on the investor. An investment manager can make an ESG Disclosure Statement available to investors in a variety of ways, such as (1) providing the ESG Disclosure Statement directly to an individual investor in a one-on-one meeting or sending an electronic version to an email address provided by the investor; (2) posting the ESG Disclosure Statement on a public or limited-access webpage accessible to investors; or (3) incorporating the ESG Disclosure Statement into regulatory documents that are required to be provided to investors prior to making an initial investment or a commitment to invest in the investment product. When the investment product is offered through a distributor or advisor, providing the ESG Disclosure Statement to the distributor or advisor satisfies Provision 1.A.9. Investment managers should consider providing an investment product's ESG Disclosure Statement to investors along with any other marketing materials for the investment product.

The investment manager's application of the ESG Disclosure Standards to its investment products is voluntary. If an investment manager no longer wishes to apply the ESG Disclosure Standards to a particular investment product, the investment manager will cease to update, maintain, and make available to investors the applicable ESG Disclosure Statement. If an investment manager no longer wishes to apply the ESG Disclosure Standards to any of its investment products, the investment manager will cease to update, maintain, and make available all of its ESG Disclosure Statements and must promptly notify CFA Institute.

Provision 1.A.10

The INVESTMENT MANAGER MUST update an INVESTMENT PRODUCT'S ESG DISCLOSURE STATEMENT when:

a. changes are made to applicable Global ESG Disclosure Standards for Investment Products REQUIREMENTS OR INTERPRETIVE GUIDANCE.

Discussion

When a change is made to the ESG Disclosure Standards requirements or interpretive guidance that affects an ESG Disclosure Statement, the ESG Disclosure Statement must be updated to comply with the updated requirements or interpretive guidance. It is expected that changes to the ESG Disclosure Standards will be infrequent. When any such changes are made, an effective date will be chosen that allows investment managers sufficient time to comply with the changes and to revise any affected ESG Disclosure Statements.

Provision 1.A.10

The INVESTMENT MANAGER MUST update an INVESTMENT PRODUCT'S ESG DISCLOSURE STATEMENT when:

b. the INVESTMENT MANAGER makes changes that affect information included in an ESG DISCLOSURE STATEMENT.

Discussion

If an investment manager makes a change to an investment product that affects the information included in that investment product's ESG Disclosure Statement, the investment manager must update the ESG Disclosure Statement. The value and relevance of the new information are affected by the timeliness with which the ESG Disclosure Statement is updated. Therefore, the investment manager must update the ESG Disclosure Statement on a timely basis.

Provision 1.A.10

The INVESTMENT MANAGER MUST update an INVESTMENT PRODUCT'S ESG DISCLOSURE STATEMENT when:

c. a significant error is found after the ESG DISCLOSURE STATEMENT is made available to INVESTORS.

Discussion

Investment managers are likely to face situations in which errors in an ESG Disclosure Statement are discovered and must be specifically addressed. Even with the tightest of controls, errors may occur. When an ESG Disclosure Statement is found to have a significant error, the ESG Disclosure Statement must be corrected. The omission of any required information from an ESG Disclosure Statement is considered a significant error. The inclusion of incorrect information in an ESG Disclosure Statement also is considered a significant error if it is probable that the incorrect information would influence a typical investor's decision to invest in the investment product. Provision 2.A.1.f contains additional disclosure requirements for significant errors.

B. Fundamentals of Compliance—Recommendations

Provision 1.B.1

The INVESTMENT MANAGER SHOULD obtain independent assurance on its ESG DISCLOSURE STATEMENTS.

Discussion

It is recommended that an investment manager obtain independent assurance on its ESG Disclosure Statements. Independent assurance is a process by which an independent third party tests one or more ESG Disclosure Statements in accordance with the required independent assurance procedures of the Global ESG Disclosure Standards for Investment Products. Independent assurance is intended to provide an investment manager and investors with additional confidence in the investment manager's claim that an ESG Disclosure Statement complies with the Global ESG Disclosure Standards for Investment Products.

Independent assurance may increase the investment manager's knowledge regarding the ESG Disclosure Standards and may also lead to improved internal policies and procedures. In addition, independent assurance may improve the quality and consistency of the investment manager's investment product disclosures and may result in a marketing advantage for the investment manager.

All requirements and recommendations related to independent assurance (other than Provision 1.B.1) for investment managers and firms conducting assurance engagements can be found in separate assurance procedures for the Global ESG Disclosure Standards for Investment Products.

2. INVESTMENT PRODUCT ESG DISCLOSURES

A. Investment Product ESG Disclosures—Requirements

General Investment Product Disclosures

Provision 2.A.1

If the INVESTMENT MANAGER chooses to apply the Global ESG Disclosure Standards for Investment Products to a specific INVESTMENT PRODUCT, the INVESTMENT MANAGER MUST prepare an ESG DISCLOSURE STATEMENT for that specific INVESTMENT PRODUCT that includes:

a. the name of the INVESTMENT PRODUCT;

b. the name of the INVESTMENT MANAGER;

c. the applicable disclosures REQUIRED by the Global ESG Disclosure Standards for Investment Products, except for any disclosures prohibited by law or regulation;

d. the period covered by the ESG DISCLOSURE STATEMENT;

e. a description of any changes made during the period covered by the ESG DISCLOSURE STATEMENT that are relevant to the applicable disclosures REQUIRED by the Global ESG Disclosure Standards for Investment Products, along with the effective dates of those changes;

f. a description of any changes made to the ESG DISCLOSURE STATEMENT within the past year to correct a significant error; and

g. the following statement:

"This ESG Disclosure Statement for [Insert period covered by the ESG DISCLOSURE STATEMENT] complies with the disclosure requirements of the Global ESG Disclosure Standards for Investment Products. Additionally, [Insert name of INVESTMENT MANAGER] has complied with the requirements of the Global ESG Disclosure Standards for Investment Products related to the preparation and presentation of this ESG Disclosure Statement.

The Global ESG Disclosure Standards for Investment Products are developed and maintained by CFA Institute. CFA Institute does not endorse or promote this organization, nor does it warrant the accuracy or quality of the content contained herein."

Discussion

An ESG Disclosure Statement may cover a single investment product or multiple investment products. If an investment manager chooses to create a single ESG Disclosure Statement that covers multiple investment products, all required disclosures must be included for each investment product. The investment manager must make clear which disclosures pertain to which investment products. If multiple investment products are included in an ESG Disclosure Statement, all uses of the term "investment product" in the ESG Disclosure Standards must be interpreted as plural.

Provision 2.A.1

If the INVESTMENT MANAGER chooses to apply the Global ESG Disclosure Standards for Investment Products to a specific INVESTMENT PRODUCT, the INVESTMENT MANAGER MUST prepare an ESG DISCLOSURE STATEMENT for that specific INVESTMENT PRODUCT that includes:

a. the name of the INVESTMENT PRODUCT.

Discussion

An ESG Disclosure Statement provides investors with information about a specific investment product. The name of the investment product must be included within the ESG Disclosure Statement.

Provision 2.A.1

If the INVESTMENT MANAGER chooses to apply the Global ESG Disclosure Standards for Investment Products to a specific INVESTMENT PRODUCT, the INVESTMENT MANAGER MUST prepare an ESG DISCLOSURE STATEMENT for that specific INVESTMENT PRODUCT that includes:

b. the name of the INVESTMENT MANAGER.

Discussion

The investment manager of an investment product is the entity that has control over determining the investment product's objectives, constraints, benchmark, policies, and approaches—collectively, the "investment strategy." When an investment manager uses a sub-advisor to implement an investment strategy, the investment manager may prepare an ESG Disclosure Statement for the investment product as long as the investment manager controls the investment strategy and selects the sub-advisor. Therefore, it is the investment manager's name, and not the name of the sub-advisor, that must be disclosed in an ESG Disclosure Statement for a sub-advised investment product. The compliance statement required by Provision 2.A.1.g must include the investment manager's name.

Provision 2.A.1

If the INVESTMENT MANAGER chooses to apply the Global ESG Disclosure Standards for Investment Products to a specific INVESTMENT PRODUCT, the INVESTMENT MANAGER MUST prepare an ESG DISCLOSURE STATEMENT for that specific INVESTMENT PRODUCT that includes:

c. the applicable disclosures REQUIRED by the Global ESG Disclosure Standards for Investment Products, except for any disclosures prohibited by law or regulation.

Discussion

When preparing an ESG Disclosure Statement for an investment product, an investment manager must include all required disclosures that pertain to that investment product. However, when a law or regulation prohibits a disclosure required by the ESG Disclosure Standards, the investment manager must adhere to the law or regulation. In such instances, an ESG Disclosure Statement can still comply with the ESG Disclosure Standards provided that the investment manager includes a description of the prohibited disclosure requirement and explains why it cannot be included, as required by Provision 2.A.2.

Provision 2.A.1

If the INVESTMENT MANAGER chooses to apply the Global ESG Disclosure Standards for Investment Products to a specific INVESTMENT PRODUCT, the INVESTMENT MANAGER MUST prepare an ESG DISCLOSURE STATEMENT for that specific INVESTMENT PRODUCT that includes:

d. the period covered by the ESG DISCLOSURE STATEMENT.

Discussion

Provision 2.A.1.d requires the period covered by the ESG Disclosure Statement to be at least one year, or the period since inception if the investment product has existed for less than one year. The disclosure of the period covered by the ESG Disclosure Statement provides investors with knowledge of the period for which the disclosures in the ESG Disclosure Statement apply to the investment product as well as a reference point for evaluating the investment product's ESG approaches. The period covered by the ESG Disclosure Statement must be included within the compliance statement required by Provision 2.A.1.g.

Sample Disclosure for a Discrete Period

"This ESG Disclosure Statement for the period from 1 January 2019 through 31 December 2021 complies with the disclosure requirements of the Global ESG Disclosure Standards for Investment Products. Additionally, XYZ Asset Management Company has complied with the requirements of the Global ESG Disclosure Standards for Investment Products related to the preparation and presentation of this ESG Disclosure Statement.

The Global ESG Disclosure Standards for Investment Products are developed and maintained by CFA Institute. CFA Institute does not endorse or promote this organization, nor does it warrant the accuracy or quality of the content contained herein."

Sample Disclosure for a Continuous Period

"This ESG Disclosure Statement complies with the disclosure requirements of the Global ESG Disclosure Standards for Investment Products for all periods beginning on or after 1 January 2019. Additionally, XYZ Asset Management Company has complied with the requirements of the Global ESG Disclosure Standards for Investment Products related to the preparation and presentation of this ESG Disclosure Statement.

The Global ESG Disclosure Standards for Investment Products are developed and maintained by CFA Institute. CFA Institute does not endorse or promote this organization, nor does it warrant the accuracy or quality of the content contained herein."

Provision 2.A.1

If the INVESTMENT MANAGER chooses to apply the Global ESG Disclosure Standards for Investment Products to a specific INVESTMENT PRODUCT, the INVESTMENT MANAGER MUST prepare an ESG DISCLOSURE STATEMENT for that specific INVESTMENT PRODUCT that includes:

e. a description of any changes made during the period covered by the ESG DISCLOSURE STATEMENT that are relevant to the applicable disclosures REQUIRED by the Global ESG Disclosure Standards for Investment Products, along with the effective dates of those changes.

Discussion

Provision 2.A.1.e requires an investment manager to describe any changes relevant to the applicable disclosures required by the ESG Disclosure Standards that were made to the investment product during the period covered by the ESG Disclosure Statement, along with the dates those changes took effect. Provision 2.A.1.e covers not only changes made to the investment product's ESG approaches and ESG-related objectives, investment process, or stewardship activities but also all changes relevant to the disclosures within the ESG Disclosure Statement that apply to the investment product, such as information about an ESG index or how certain information is reported to investors.

Sample Disclosure 1

"The Strategy's investment policy was amended as of 1 January 2020 to exclude companies deriving any revenues from thermal coal mining and coal power generation."

Sample Disclosure 2

"On 1 April 2021, we modified our fundamental analysis process to systematically identify and analyze ESG information that is relevant to the risk and return of an investment over the target holding period for that investment. Prior to this date, ESG exclusionary screening was the only ESG approach used in the Fund's investment process."

Sample Disclosure 3

"Prior to 1 March 2019, we provided a summary of stewardship activities to clients annually by email. Subsequently, we post on our website a quarterly investment stewardship report that is available at www.xyzfirm.com/stewardship."

Provision 2.A.1

If the INVESTMENT MANAGER chooses to apply the Global ESG Disclosure Standards for Investment Products to a specific INVESTMENT PRODUCT, the INVESTMENT MANAGER MUST prepare an ESG DISCLOSURE STATEMENT for that specific INVESTMENT PRODUCT that includes:

f. a description of any changes made to the ESG DISCLOSURE STATEMENT within the past year to correct a significant error.

Discussion

When an investment manager has corrected a significant error in an ESG Disclosure Statement, the investment manager must disclose a description of the changes made to the ESG Disclosure Statement to correct the error. After one year, the investment manager may remove this disclosure from the ESG Disclosure Statement.

Provision 2.A.1

If the INVESTMENT MANAGER chooses to apply the Global ESG Disclosure Standards for Investment Products to a specific INVESTMENT PRODUCT, the INVESTMENT MANAGER MUST prepare an ESG DISCLOSURE STATEMENT for that specific INVESTMENT PRODUCT that includes:

g. the following statement:

"This ESG Disclosure Statement for [Insert period covered by the ESG DISCLOSURE STATEMENT] complies with the disclosure requirements of the Global ESG Disclosure Standards for Investment Products. Additionally, [Insert name of INVESTMENT MANAGER] has complied with the requirements of the Global ESG Disclosure Standards for Investment Products related to the preparation and presentation of this ESG Disclosure Statement.

The Global ESG Disclosure Standards for Investment Products are developed and maintained by CFA Institute. CFA Institute does not endorse or promote this organization, nor does it warrant the accuracy or quality of the content contained herein."

Discussion

An ESG Disclosure Statement must include the compliance statement shown in Provision 2.A.1.g. The English version of the compliance statement is the controlling version. An investment manager may translate the compliance statement into a language for which there is no official translation of the ESG Disclosure Standards. When doing so, however, the investment manager must ensure that the translation reflects the required wording of the compliance statement in Provision 2.A.1.g.

The language in the compliance statement must not exclude any portion of the respective compliance statement. In some instances, however, it may be appropriate for an investment manager to modify the language slightly. For example, an investment manager may need to modify the language to add details about the name of the investment manager that manages the investment product or when multiple investment products are included within a single ESG Disclosure Statement.

Provision 2.A.2

If an INVESTMENT MANAGER is prohibited by law or regulation from making a REQUIRED disclosure in the ESG DISCLOSURE STATEMENT, then the INVESTMENT MANAGER MUST disclose a description of the REQUIRED disclosure that cannot be included and explain why it cannot be included.

Discussion

In some instances, a disclosure required by the ESG Disclosure Standards may be prohibited by law or regulation. In such cases, the investment product's ESG Disclosure Statement may still comply with the ESG Disclosure Standards provided that the investment manager includes a description of the prohibited disclosure requirement in the ESG Disclosure Statement along with an explanation of why the required disclosure cannot be included.

Sample Disclosure

"Country A Regulation 123 prohibits investment managers from advertising an investment product's compliance with international third-party labels or certifications that have not been properly registered in Country A. Whereas this investment product complies with the requirements of one such third-party labeling program, and this compliance is advertised when this product is marketed in other countries, the information about the third-party label that is required by the Global ESG Disclosures Standards for Investment Products is not included in this ESG Disclosure Statement, which is provided to investors in Country A."

Provision 2.A.3

The INVESTMENT MANAGER MUST disclose a summary description of the ESG APPROACHES used in the INVESTMENT PRODUCT.

Discussion

The ESG Disclosure Standards define an ESG approach as one of a variety of methods for incorporating ESG considerations into an investment product's objectives, investment process, or stewardship activities. This term includes but is not limited to approaches that are often referred to as ESG integration, exclusion, screening, best-in-class, thematic, sustainability themed investing, impact investing, and stewardship.

The summary description of the ESG approaches used in the investment product will help investors understand the methods an investment manager uses to incorporate ESG considerations into the investment product's objectives, investment process, or stewardship activities. When preparing the summary description of the ESG approaches used in the investment product, investment managers are encouraged to review Section 3 of the ESG Disclosure Standards, titled "ESG Terminology," which provides recommendations for using ESG terminology in an ESG Disclosure Statement.

Sample Disclosure 1

"The XYZ Equity Strategy (the 'Strategy') uses ESG integration—the systematic and explicit inclusion of material environmental, social, and governance (ESG) data in financial analysis—in its pursuit of long-term capital growth. We consider financially material ESG data to be part of a comprehensive analysis of security risk and valuation. The XYZ Asset Management ('XYZ') ESG analysis and integration process applies to all equity securities; ESG data are not considered for the Strategy's money market securities.

The Strategy excludes certain types of investments that XYZ believes contribute to environmental or social harm. In addition, the Strategy excludes investments in companies that derive revenue from thermal coal mining and coal power generation because XYZ believes the coal industry is at significant economic risk as the world transitions to a lower-carbon economy.

In its stewardship activities, XYZ considers ESG issues that are financially relevant to a company when voting proxies and engaging the management of that company."

Sample Disclosure 2

"The Fund intends to attain a positive, measurable environmental impact through direct equity investments in enterprises that provide solutions to protect and restore fragile ecosystems.

Potential investee companies that we deem to be in violation of our Responsible Investing Policy exclusionary screening criteria will not be considered for investment. In addition to supplying capital to investee companies, the firm seeks to influence investee company policies and decisions related to ecosystem protection and restoration by obtaining seats on investee company governance boards."

Provision 2.A.4

If the INVESTMENT PRODUCT's investment process, STEWARDSHIP ACTIVITIES, or objectives systematically address one or more specific ESG issues, then the INVESTMENT MANAGER MUST disclose a summary description of those specific ESG issues.

Discussion

A summary description of the specific ESG issues that are systematically addressed in the investment product's investment process, stewardship activities, or objectives will help investors determine if an investment product addresses an ESG issue in which they have a particular interest. Examples of such ESG issues include climate change, biodiversity, gender diversity, and faith-based values. Investment managers need not list all ESG issues considered in the investment product's investment process, stewardship activities, or objectives; only specific ESG issues that are systematically addressed must be disclosed.

Not all investment products with ESG approaches are designed to systematically address specific ESG issues. If an investment product's ESG approach does not systematically address any specific ESG issues, Provision 2.A.4 does not apply.

Sample Disclosure

"Sustainability is an important consideration for the ABC Growth and Income Fund. ABC Fund Management defines sustainability as 'the responsible and efficient consumption and management of natural resources that allow future generations to meet their own needs.' One of the most important sustainability issues is the burning of fossil fuels and the resulting negative effect on global warming. ABC Fund Management believes that companies that use fossil fuels efficiently or transition to renewable energy sources not only ensure their own continuity but also contribute to a more sustainable economy."

Provision 2.A.5

The INVESTMENT MANAGER MUST disclose any third-party ESG-related labels and certifications with which the INVESTMENT PRODUCT complies.

Discussion

ESG-related labels and certifications can be efficient mechanisms for communicating to investors that an investment product has certain ESG approaches, meets certain minimum standards, or has undergone some form of independent review. Investment managers must disclose the ESG-related labels and certifications with which the investment product complies.

Provision 2.A.5 applies only to ESG-related labels and certifications with which the investment product complies. It does not apply to any ESG-related codes and standards with which the investment manager, as an entity, complies. Such information may be of interest to investors, however, and investment managers may include this information in an ESG Disclosure Statement if they so choose.

Sample Disclosure

"The Fund has been awarded the Febelfin Towards Sustainability label. Information about the Towards Sustainability label, including a list of funds that have been awarded the label, may be viewed at the Febelfin website (www.towardssustainability.be)."

Sources and Types of ESG Information

Provision 2.A.6

If ESG information is used in an INVESTMENT PRODUCT'S investment process or STEWARDSHIP ACTIVITIES, then the INVESTMENT MANAGER MUST disclose:

a. the elements of the investment process or STEWARDSHIP ACTIVITIES that use ESG information and how the ESG information is used;
b. a description of the type of ESG information used and a description of the sources from which that ESG information is obtained; and
c. the risks and limitations of the ESG information used and how those risks and limitations are managed.

Discussion

The ESG Disclosure Standards consider ESG information to be environmental, social, or governance information used in an investment product's investment process or stewardship activities. Various types of ESG information exist, including but not limited to ESG ratings and scores; ESG-related observations, statistics, metrics, and measures; and qualitative ESG information.

Provision 2.A.6

If ESG information is used in an INVESTMENT PRODUCT'S investment process or STEWARDSHIP ACTIVITIES, then the INVESTMENT MANAGER MUST disclose:

a. the elements of the investment process or STEWARDSHIP ACTIVITIES that use ESG information and how the ESG information is used.

Discussion

ESG information can be used in many different elements of an investment product's investment process or stewardship activities. For instance, ESG information may inform asset allocation, research and analysis, security selection, portfolio construction, proxy voting, and engagement efforts. ESG information can also be used in many different ways in an investment product. As an example, financially material ESG information may be used in security analysis and valuation. In another example, ESG information may be used in the portfolio construction process to exclude securities that violate certain faith-based principles. Provision 2.A.6.a requires an investment manager to disclose which elements of an investment product's investment process or stewardship activities use ESG information and how the ESG information is used.

Sample Disclosure 1

"The Global Equity Strategy uses ESG information to exclude securities that are deemed to violate OECD Guidelines for Multinational Enterprises, help identify material financial risks in security analysis and selection, inform proxy voting decisions, and identify material ESG issues for engagement efforts."

Sample Disclosure 2

"Security selection begins with ranking companies in the Fund's universe within their industries according to their carbon intensity and then analyzing the feasibility of using engagement to facilitate a meaningful reduction in company greenhouse gas emissions."

Provision 2.A.6

If ESG information is used in an INVESTMENT PRODUCT's investment process or STEWARDSHIP ACTIVITIES, then the INVESTMENT MANAGER MUST disclose:

b. a description of the type of ESG information used and a description of the sources from which that ESG information is obtained.

Discussion

An investment manager is required to describe the types and the sources of the ESG information used in the investment product's investment process or stewardship activities. For example, an investment manager might use ESG risk ratings from a third-party data provider to assess a company's environmental risks. Another investment manager might use statistics, metrics, and measures from company disclosures, government organizations, and industry organizations to assess the company's environmental risks. Investment managers are not required to disclose details about the specific ESG information used in an investment product's investment process or stewardship activities, but they may provide examples of such information if they so choose.

Sources of ESG information include but are not limited to the following:

- regulatory filings,
- financial reports,
- corporate sustainability/responsibility reports,
- issuer calls, meetings, and presentations,
- site visits,
- customer and supplier interviews ("channel checks"),
- ESG data providers,
- industry trade organizations,
- government records, and
- news reports.

An investment manager may choose, but is not required, to disclose the names of its ESG data providers when describing its sources of ESG information. If an investment manager obtains ESG information from an ESG data provider, it is sufficient to state that the ESG information comes from an ESG data provider.

Sample Disclosure 1

"Our analysts calculate proprietary governance scores for companies in our security selection universe based on company-disclosed corporate governance data that we collect. This data includes but is not limited to board composition ratios and metrics, board structure, shareholder voting rights, and ethical violations."

Sample Disclosure 2

"We use external vendors and non-profit organizations to obtain Scope 1, Scope 2, and Scope 3 emissions and carbon intensity for companies in the Fund's investment universe."

Provision 2.A.6

If ESG information is used in an INVESTMENT PRODUCT's investment process or STEWARDSHIP ACTIVITIES, then the INVESTMENT MANAGER MUST disclose:

c. the risks and limitations of the ESG information used and how those risks and limitations are managed.

Discussion

The accuracy, consistency, and comparability of ESG information can vary greatly, introducing risks and limitations to its use. Such risks and limitations include but are not limited to making investment decisions or measuring portfolio characteristics based on inaccurate or incomplete information. As an example, total carbon emissions data—that is, Scope 1, 2, and 3 issuer emissions—may be unavailable for all securities held in a portfolio, thus creating a risk that portfolio climate change scenarios and related investment decisions are made based on an incomplete dataset.

Factors that an investment manager should consider when determining the risks and limitations of the ESG information that is used in the investment product include but are not limited to the following:

- the type of ESG information;
- the degree of standardization in the way the ESG information is defined and measured;
- the degree of skill and judgment required to collect, measure, and interpret the ESG information;
- timing lags between company disclosures and third-party data provider inclusion;
- the completeness of the ESG information dataset; and
- the reliance on estimated or modeled ESG information.

Provision 2.A.6.c also requires an investment manager to disclose how it manages the risks and limitations of the ESG information used in an investment product. Some examples of such efforts include evaluating the quality of ESG data, establishing policies for managing incomplete or inconsistent datasets, and conducting due diligence on ESG data providers.

Sample Disclosure 1

"XYZ Asset Management ('XYZ') has conducted due diligence on the data collection and data governance processes of its ESG data providers. Because ESG data quality can be inconsistent, data samples from external sources are cross-referenced quarterly against company-disclosed data, against other original source data, and between ESG data vendors. Acceptable data variance limits are determined per type of data by XYZ's data scientists. Financially material ESG data for some companies may be unavailable or may fail to meet our data quality standards. In these cases, the weight of the company in the portfolio will not exceed 1% of the portfolio's market value, and the weight of all such companies in the portfolio will not exceed 10% of the portfolio's market value."

Sample Disclosure 2

"ABC Fund Management ('ABC') measures the carbon intensity of our portfolio companies. A company's Scope 1 and Scope 2 greenhouse gas emissions and revenue are used to calculate its carbon intensity. Not all companies report their greenhouse gas emissions; thus, carbon intensity estimates for individual companies can vary greatly among data providers. ABC has chosen a data provider that obtains greenhouse gas emissions data from multiple sources (including company-reported data, third-party data, and its own proprietary estimates); whose combined Scope 1 and Scope 2 company emissions estimates have been demonstrated to correlate well with those of other data providers; and whose estimation methods generally align with guidance from Greenhouse Gas Protocol."

Systematic Consideration of Financially Material ESG Information in Investment Decisions

Provision 2.A.7

If financially material ESG information is systematically considered in investment decisions, then the INVESTMENT MANAGER MUST disclose:

a. how financially material ESG information is typically identified;
b. how financially material ESG information is typically incorporated into investment decisions, differentiated by type of investment when necessary; and
c. exceptions in which financially material ESG information is not considered in investment decisions, if any.

Discussion

Financially material ESG information is ESG information that is relevant to the assessment of the risk and return of an investment or a portfolio of investments as determined by the investment manager through research, analysis, and judgment. To systematically consider financially material ESG information in investment decisions means to consider such information in a regular, consistent, and methodical manner in the investment decision-making process. It is acknowledged that financial materiality can change over time; that is, some ESG information that an investment manager considers to be financially material today may not be considered financially material in the future, and vice versa. It is also acknowledged that financially material ESG information is contextual in nature, and it is unlikely that a single set of ESG information is financially material to all research, analysis, or investment decisions for an investment product. Therefore, an investment manager is not expected to provide details about the specific financially material ESG information used in its research, analysis, or investment decision-making for an investment product, although an investment manager may provide this information or examples of such information if it chooses to do so.

Provision 2.A.7

If financially material ESG information is systematically considered in investment decisions, then the INVESTMENT MANAGER MUST disclose:

a. how financially material ESG information is typically identified.

Discussion

Provision 2.A.7.a requires an investment manager to disclose how it typically distinguishes ESG information that is financially material to investment decisions for an investment product from ESG information that is immaterial for that investment product. For example, an investment manager might describe its use of a third-party framework, such as the Sustainability Accounting Standards Board (SASB) Standards; its internal research and analysis processes; or its use of third-party research and analysis.

Sample Disclosure 1

"Our sector analysts are responsible for identifying material ESG factors for the companies they cover. They begin by referencing the Sustainability Accounting Standards Board (SASB) Standards. These standards are used to identify ESG issues that are most relevant to financial performance based on the industry in which a company operates. Relevant ESG issues are identified per industry, and our sector analysts consider industry-relevant SASB metrics for each company. This analysis is supplemented by an analysis of a company's unique characteristics, such as its geographic location, which may also contribute to material ESG factors.

Certain material corporate governance issues are evaluated for each company. These issues include board structure, independence, and composition; board director skill sets and experience levels; executive remuneration; and shareholder voting rights.

Finally, ESG factor materiality is assessed based on the analyst's estimated investment horizon for an individual security. If an ESG factor is projected to have a negative short-term material effect on a company's valuation, the security may still be purchased or held if the analyst's investment horizon exceeds the projected short-term effect. Conversely, an ESG factor that is expected to have positive material benefits for a company over the long term will not be considered in the valuation of that security if the analyst's investment horizon for the security is short."

Sample Disclosure 2

"As a manager of multifactor investment products, we rely on statistical techniques to identify correlations between factors and price movements that can lead to alpha generation or risk reduction. Our valuation model integrates a proprietary governance factor alongside momentum, quality, and value factors. Because ESG scores differ among data providers, we conducted a regression of eight governance sub-scores per provider that we believed were likely to affect a company's performance and that are based on information widely disclosed by issuers. We regressed the sub-scores against the historical returns of the portfolio's benchmark. Based on the regression results, we combined statistically robust sub-scores to create a proprietary governance factor used in our valuation models."

Provision 2.A.7

If financially material ESG information is systematically considered in investment decisions, then the INVESTMENT MANAGER MUST disclose:

b. how financially material ESG information is typically incorporated into investment decisions, differentiated by type of investment when necessary.

Discussion

Investment managers use a variety of techniques to incorporate financially material ESG information in investment decisions. Some techniques apply only to certain types of investments, such as equities, fixed income, or real estate. Other techniques apply only to certain types of investment decisions—that is, particular steps of the investment process such as asset allocation, portfolio construction, security selection, security analysis, or risk management. For example:

- In asset allocation and portfolio construction, techniques include scenario analysis, sensitivity analysis, and benchmark-relative weighting.
- In equity security analysis, techniques include adjustments to forecasted financials and financial ratios, valuation model assumptions, and valuation multiples.
- In fixed-income security analysis, techniques include adjustments to forecasted financials and financial ratios, credit quality assessments, and credit spreads.

Provision 2.A.7.b requires an investment manager to disclose information about the specific techniques it uses to systematically consider financially material ESG information in its investment decisions for the investment product. This disclosure must be differentiated by type of investment if a specific technique does not apply to all types of investments in the investment product.

Sample Disclosure 1

"Quantitative and qualitative ESG data that we judge to be material to a security's future financial performance are considered by XYZ's sector analysts alongside other material information when assessing historical company performance, making financial statement estimates and adjustments, and comparing the company with its industry peers. Our analysts also assess how well a company understands and manages the identified ESG risks. In addition, XYZ has developed a proprietary regression model to estimate the impact of a company's governance factors on its projected performance. Our analysts may use the output from this model to raise or lower their estimated risk premium for a company."

Sample Disclosure 2

"Our top-down, bottom-up fixed-income investment process begins with 1-year, 5-year, and 10-year interest rate forecasts derived from our proprietary interest rate model. Our 5-year and 10-year forecasts incorporate a climate change scenario analysis that is quantified as a risk factor in the model for these time horizons. Our credit analysts incorporate material quantitative ESG factors that have been identified as contributors to near-term or long-term issuer credit risk into their credit analysis to determine effects on issuer profitability, leverage, cash flow coverage, and other credit ratios. Relative credit spreads are determined based on our assessment of issuer creditworthiness. A security's credit spread may at times be widened or narrowed based on qualitative material ESG factors, such as governance risk or headline risk. Our fixed-income portfolio seeks to generate long-term attractive risk-adjusted returns and is diversified by sector and 1-, 5-, and 10-year investment time horizons."

Provision 2.A.7

If financially material ESG information is systematically considered in investment decisions, then the INVESTMENT MANAGER MUST disclose:

c. exceptions in which financially material ESG information is not considered in investment decisions.

Discussion

If an investment manager does not consider financially material ESG information in all types of investment decisions for the investment product, the investment manager must describe the circumstances in which financially material ESG information is not considered. For example, the investment manager might consider financially material ESG information in the analysis of only certain types of securities. If so, the types of securities for which financially material ESG information is not considered in investment decisions must be disclosed.

Sample Disclosure 1

"The consideration of financially material ESG information is part of our credit analysis and valuation process for all fixed-income securities except US Treasury securities."

Sample Disclosure 2

"Financially material ESG factors are analyzed for a minimum of 90% of the market value of the investment product's holdings. Financially material ESG factors are not analyzed for money market holdings, which may constitute up to 10% of the investment product's market value."

ESG Investment Universe

Provision 2.A.8

If the INVESTMENT PRODUCT uses an ESG INDEX as an investment universe, then the INVESTMENT MANAGER MUST disclose:

a. either the significant ESG characteristics of the index or, if the index is a readily recognized index, the name of the index; and
b. how an INVESTOR can obtain information about the index construction methodology.

Discussion

The ESG Disclosure Standards define an ESG index as an index that includes ESG considerations in its index construction methodology. An ESG index can be constructed in a variety of ways, such as by applying ESG screening criteria or ESG considerations to an underlying index universe or parent index. ESG indexes also may be constructed for a variety of purposes, such as to achieve certain index-level ESG characteristics while maintaining sector and geographic weightings similar to those of the parent index or to focus on a specific ESG theme or issue. Paris-aligned and climate transition benchmarks are also considered ESG indexes under the ESG Disclosure Standards. ESG indexes can serve as the investment universe for both actively managed and passively managed investment products.

Provision 2.A.8

If the INVESTMENT PRODUCT uses an ESG INDEX as an investment universe, then the INVESTMENT MANAGER MUST disclose:

a. either the significant ESG characteristics of the index or, if the index is a readily recognized index, the name of the index.

Discussion

A significant ESG index characteristic is an index characteristic based on ESG issues or ESG information that is likely to be of importance to an investor when choosing an investment product that uses an ESG index as its investment universe. Some examples of types of significant ESG characteristics of an ESG index include but are not limited to:

- specific ESG themes, such as gender diversity;
- ESG statistics, measurements, or metrics, such as carbon footprint or carbon efficiency;
- ESG-related exclusions; and
- the use of ESG scores or ratings in constituent selection.

If the ESG index is a readily recognized index, providing the ESG index name will satisfy Provision 2.A.8.a. Each investment manager must decide for itself whether an index is readily recognized. If the investment manager is uncertain as to whether the ESG index is readily recognized, the investment manager must describe the significant ESG characteristics of the index.

Sample Disclosure 1

"The Global Gender Diversity Index is composed of companies that have at least one of the following characteristics: a female CEO or board chairperson, 30% or more women on its executive management team, or 30% or more women on its governing board."

Sample Disclosure 2

"The XYZ Climate Index ('Index') is compatible with a 1.5-degree Celsius global warming climate scenario through the selection and weighting of its constituent securities. The Index is a subset of the XYZ Broad Market Equity Index. The Index is designed to meet the minimum standards for methodology of an 'EU Paris-Aligned' benchmark. The Index places a limit on exposure to companies that do not disclose their carbon emissions and applies constituent weighting caps to limit the Index's exposure to the physical and transition risks of climate change. The Index is constructed to have lower measures of greenhouse gas emissions and fossil fuel reserves than the XYZ Broad Market Equity Index. All Index constituents must be aligned with a transition pathway toward a 1.5-degree Celsius climate warming scenario. The Index excludes companies that generate revenue from coal, oil, or natural gas exploration or processing."

Provision 2.A.8

If the INVESTMENT PRODUCT uses an ESG INDEX as an investment universe, then the INVESTMENT MANAGER MUST disclose:

b. how an INVESTOR can obtain information about the index construction methodology.

Discussion

An index construction methodology is a set of rules or criteria that are applied to the constituent selection process, the calculation of index values, and the maintenance of the index. The index construction methodology can provide investors with information that may be relevant to their decision whether or not to invest in the investment product. Examples of such information include but are not limited to:

- a description of the ESG criteria that are applied to constituent selection;
- how the ESG criteria are used in constituent selection, such as a best-in-class or positive screening methodology;
- exceptions to the ESG selection criteria; and
- the application of systematic ESG exclusions.

When an ESG index is used as an investment universe, Provision 2.A.8.b requires the investment manager to disclose how investors can obtain information about the ESG index construction methodology. This disclosure may take several forms, such as the provision of an index webpage address or an embedded link in the ESG Disclosure Statement that will lead investors to the required information.

Sample Disclosure

"Information about the XYZ Climate Index is available on the website of the Index Administrator, XYZ Index Creator AG."

Screening

Provision 2.A.9

If an INVESTMENT PRODUCT has ESG[2] criteria that systematically exclude certain investments or has ESG criteria that need to be met in order for an investment to be considered for inclusion in the portfolio, then the INVESTMENT MANAGER MUST disclose for each ESG criterion:

a. the characteristic of the investment that is evaluated;
b. the threshold or condition against which the characteristic is compared;
c. whether the investment is excluded from, or is eligible for inclusion in, the portfolio when the threshold or condition is met; and
d. a reference, where applicable, to any law, regulation, or third-party standard, guideline, or framework used in the establishment or evaluation of the ESG criterion.

Discussion

Provision 2.A.9 applies when an investment product has screening criteria that are based on ESG information or ESG issues and that are systematically applied at the investment level. To systematically apply investment-level ESG screening criteria means to apply the ESG screening criteria in a regular, consistent, and methodical manner to all investments considered in the investment decision-making process. When determining whether screening criteria are systematically applied, an investment manager may want to consider whether:

- the screening criteria are described in the investment agreement, prospectus, or other legal documents that govern the investment product;

[2] The Global ESG Disclosure Standards for Investment Products incorrectly omitted the acronym "ESG" from the language in Provision 2.A.9. Provision 2.A.9 as stated here is correct.

- the investment manager would notify investors prior to making a change to the screening criteria;
- the screening criteria would remain in effect during favorable and unfavorable investment conditions; or
- the screening criteria are required by law or regulation.

A criterion is not systematically applied if the investment manager has discretion to apply the criterion; that is, if there are no policies governing the application or suspension of the systematic screening for the criterion. For example, an exclusion criterion is not systematically applied if an investment manager can decide to purchase one or more securities that violate the exclusion criterion.

Screening criteria that are not based on ESG information or ESG issues do not trigger Provision 2.A.9. For example, consider a large-cap fund that excludes all investments with a market cap below a predetermined threshold. The purpose of the exclusion is unrelated to an ESG issue, and the criterion is evaluated based on a traditional financial characteristic. Thus, this exclusion thus does not trigger Provision 2.A.9.

Provision 2.A.9

If an INVESTMENT PRODUCT has ESG criteria that systematically exclude certain investments or has ESG criteria that need to be met in order for an investment to be considered for inclusion in the portfolio, then the INVESTMENT MANAGER MUST disclose for each ESG criterion:

a. the characteristic of the investment that is evaluated.

Discussion

The disclosure of an ESG screening criterion must include the investment characteristic that is evaluated when determining whether the investment is to be excluded from or considered for inclusion in the portfolio. Examples of such characteristics include the manufacture, distribution, or sale of certain products or services; norms violations or involvement in controversies; ESG scores or ratings; and security-specific environmental or social characteristics.

Provision 2.A.9

If an INVESTMENT PRODUCT has ESG criteria that systematically exclude certain investments or has ESG criteria that need to be met in order for an investment to be considered for inclusion in the portfolio, then the INVESTMENT MANAGER MUST disclose for each ESG criterion:

b. the threshold or condition against which the characteristic is compared.

Discussion

An investment manager must disclose the threshold or condition of the investment characteristic that must be met in order for an investment to be excluded from or considered for inclusion in the portfolio. When a characteristic is measured quantitatively, the threshold must be described quantitatively—for example, "a company's greenhouse gas intensity shall not exceed 150 metric tons per €M revenue" or "no investments will be made in companies that derive more than 5% of their revenue from the production of conventional weapons and components." When a characteristic is based on a subjective assessment, the threshold must be disclosed in terms of the state, condition, or circumstance that triggers the exclusion or the consideration for inclusion. For example, "issuers that our ESG data service provider has deemed to significantly violate the OECD Guidelines for Multinational Enterprises within the past 12 months will be excluded" or "only companies that provide the potential for successful engagement, as determined by our proprietary assessment methodology, will be considered for investment." If a third party provides the criteria for subjective assessments, an investment manager must disclose whether the third party or the investment manager has the ultimate decision-making authority to determine whether the ESG-related screening criterion has been met.

Screening criteria may be based on fixed thresholds or relative thresholds. For example, an investment product might exclude all companies that do not meet a minimum requirement of 30% women in executive management roles. This criterion is an example of a fixed threshold. Another investment product might exclude all companies that fall in the bottom quartile of their peer group for the percentage of women in executive management roles. This criterion is an example of a relative threshold. Provision 2.A.9.b is not triggered based on whether the thresholds or conditions for the criteria are fixed or relative. Rather, it is triggered based on whether or not the screening criterion is systematically applied at the investment level.

If an investment product has criteria requirements or targets at the portfolio level that are based on ESG information or ESG issues, the investment manager must determine whether such criteria should be disclosed under Provision 2.A.11, Portfolio-Level ESG Characteristics, or Provision 2.A.14, Portfolio-Level Allocation Targets. As an example, an investment product that requires the portfolio to have a weighted average ESG rating of AA has a portfolio-level ESG characteristic target, which triggers the application of Provision 2.A.11. As another example, an investment product that has a target to allocate at least 80% of its market value to securities with an ESG rating of BBB or higher has a portfolio-level allocation target, which triggers the application of Provision 2.A.14.

Provision 2.A.9

If an INVESTMENT PRODUCT has ESG criteria that systematically exclude certain investments or has ESG criteria that need to be met in order for an investment to be considered for inclusion in the portfolio, then the INVESTMENT MANAGER MUST disclose for each ESG criterion:

c. whether the investment is excluded from, or is eligible for inclusion in, the portfolio when the threshold or condition is met.

Discussion

The threshold or condition against which an investment characteristic is compared can be used to either exclude certain investments from the portfolio or determine that certain investments are eligible for inclusion in the portfolio. Provision 2.A.9.c requires that an investment manager disclose whether an investment is excluded from, or eligible for inclusion in, the portfolio when the threshold or condition is met. For example, an investment manager might disclose that the portfolio excludes companies that engage in activities considered to be human rights abusive.

Provision 2.A.9

If an INVESTMENT PRODUCT has ESG criteria that systematically exclude certain investments or has ESG criteria that need to be met in order for an investment to be considered for inclusion in the portfolio, then the INVESTMENT MANAGER MUST disclose for each ESG criterion:

d. a reference, where applicable, to any law, regulation, or third-party standard, guideline, or framework used in the establishment or evaluation of the ESG criterion.

Discussion

The disclosure relating to a systematically applied ESG screening criterion must reference any law, regulation, or third-party standard, guideline, or framework used to establish or evaluate the criterion. For example, an investment product may be prohibited by law or regulation from holding certain types of investments. If a regulatory exclusion is based on ESG information or ESG issues, Provision 2.A.9.d applies.

In some cases, an investment product may be described as being compliant with a certain third-party standard, guideline, or framework. If such compliance is based on ESG information or ESG issues, such as ESG screening criteria, Provision 2.A.9.d applies.

Sample Disclosure

"The Islamic Equity Fund is compliant with Sharia law and invests according to the principles of Islamic finance."

Provision 2.A.10

If an INVESTMENT PRODUCT has ESG[3] criteria that systematically exclude certain investments or has ESG criteria that need to be met in order for an investment to be considered for inclusion in the portfolio, then the INVESTMENT MANAGER MUST disclose:

a. where the ESG criteria are applied in the investment process.

Discussion

ESG screening criteria may be used at various points in the investment process, such as when:

- narrowing the investment universe,
- identifying securities eligible for inclusion,
- monitoring investments, or
- constructing the portfolio.

Different ESG screening criteria may be applied at different points in the investment process. For example, an initial set of ESG screening criteria may be applied to exclude investments from the investment universe, and a second set of ESG screening criteria may be applied to identify securities that are eligible for inclusion. As another example, a series of exclusionary and inclusionary screens may be applied to quantitatively construct a portfolio. The investment manager must disclose at which points in the investment process it applies ESG screening criteria.

[3] The Global ESG Disclosure Standards for Investment Products incorrectly omitted the acronym "ESG" from the language in Provision 2.A.10. Provision 2.A.10.a as stated here is correct.

Sample Disclosure

"Our investment process begins with excluding from our investment universe all issuers that are deemed to be in violation of one or more UN Global Compact principles. We then apply an ESG rating screen. Securities that have an ESG rating in the top third of their sector are considered for inclusion in the portfolio."

Provision 2.A.10

If an INVESTMENT PRODUCT has ESG[4] criteria that systematically exclude certain investments or has ESG criteria that need to be met in order for an investment to be considered for inclusion in the portfolio, then the INVESTMENT MANAGER MUST disclose:

b. the exceptions to the application of the ESG criteria, if any.

Discussion

If the ESG screening criteria disclosed under Provision 2.A.9 are not applied to all investments at all times, the investment manager must disclose the circumstances when the ESG screening criteria are not applied. Examples of exceptions to the application of ESG screening criteria include when:

- the ESG screening criteria differ by type of investment,
- the data used to evaluate the ESG screening criteria is unavailable,
- override policies exist, and
- ESG screening criteria are not applied to investments that have been loaned under a securities lending agreement.

Investment managers must disclose any exceptions to the systematic application of the ESG screening criteria. For example, if an ESG screening criterion is applied to new investments but not to existing investments (that is, existing holdings are "grandfathered"), the investment manager must disclose this exception to the application of the screening criterion.

Sample Disclosure for Provisions 2.A.9. and 2.A.10

"XYZ applies exclusions to the Strategy's equity securities. Exclusions are not applied to the Strategy's money market securities. Exclusions are determined based on either industry codes or revenue thresholds. XYZ receives a monthly list from its ESG data provider of securities to be excluded from its portfolios based on the defined exclusion criteria. Exclusion criteria are applied

[4] The Global ESG Disclosure Standards for Investment Products incorrectly omitted the acronym "ESG" from the language in Provision 2.A.10. Provision 2.A.10.b as stated here is correct.

at the onset of the investment process. Securities that meet any of the criteria listed below are excluded from the security selection universe. If a current holding is subsequently found to be in violation of XYZ's exclusion criteria, the security will be sold within 60 days.

Tobacco

- Companies that have a Standard Industrial Classification (SIC) code in Major Group 21. This group includes businesses primarily engaged in manufacturing cigarettes, cigars, smoking and chewing tobacco, snuff, reconstituted tobacco, non-tobacco cigarettes, or in stemming and re-drying tobacco; or
- Companies that earned more than 5% of their annual revenue in their most recent fiscal year from the sale or distribution of cigarettes, cigars, smokeless and chewing tobacco, snuff, and non-tobacco cigarettes.

Alcohol

- Companies that have a Standard Industrial Classification (SIC) code of 2082 (Malt Beverages), 2084 (Wines, Brandy, and Brandy Spirits), or 2085 (Distilled and Blended Liquors); or
- Companies that earned more than 5% of their annual revenue from the sale or distribution of alcoholic beverages in their most recent fiscal year.

Pornography

- Companies that produce or distribute pornography. Zero tolerance revenue threshold.

Gambling

- Companies that earned more than 5% of their annual revenue in their most recent fiscal year from the offering of gambling.

Controversial Weapons

- Companies that produce, distribute, or maintain controversial weapons and key components thereof. Controversial weapons include but are not limited to cluster munitions; anti-personnel landmines; and biological, chemical, and nuclear weapons. The Strategy also complies with Regulation 123-4567, which requires the exclusion of investments in companies involved with the manufacture of cluster munitions and anti-personnel landmines. Zero tolerance revenue threshold.

Coal

- Companies that derive revenue from thermal coal mining or coal power generation. Zero tolerance revenue threshold."

Portfolio-Level ESG Characteristics

Provision 2.A.11

If the INVESTMENT PRODUCT has targets for portfolio-level ESG characteristics, then the INVESTMENT MANAGER MUST disclose for each target:

a. the portfolio-level ESG characteristic that is evaluated;
b. how the portfolio-level ESG characteristic is measured;
c. the target value or range for the portfolio-level ESG characteristic;
d. how the target portfolio-level ESG characteristic is expected to be attained;
e. the risks that could significantly hinder the attainment of the target portfolio-level ESG characteristic, should they occur; and
f. a reference, where applicable, to any law, regulation, or third-party standard, guideline, or framework used to measure the portfolio-level ESG characteristic or set the target.

Discussion

An ESG characteristic is an investment-level characteristic that is based on ESG information or ESG issues, such as a security's ESG rating or a company's carbon intensity. A portfolio-level ESG characteristic is based on an investment-level ESG characteristic that is calculated or aggregated and reported at the portfolio level, such as a weighted average ESG rating or a weighted average carbon intensity. Types of portfolio-level ESG characteristics include but are not limited to ESG-related portfolio measurements, metrics, ratios, scores, and ratings.

The existence of a portfolio-level ESG characteristic target does not imply, nor require, that each investment in the portfolio has that target portfolio-level ESG characteristic. For example, consider a portfolio that holds securities with ESG ratings ranging from BB to AAA but targets a weighted average portfolio ESG rating of AA. The ESG ratings for each security will differ, and the AA rating target is a weighted average of all security ratings. To contrast this portfolio-level ESG characteristic target with an ESG screening criterion, consider a portfolio that requires all investments to have an ESG rating of AA and excludes any investment that does not meet that requirement. In this case, the portfolio has a systematically applied investment-level exclusion criterion, which triggers Provision 2.A.9, Screening.

An investment product can have both systematically applied investment-level ESG screening criteria and portfolio-level ESG characteristic targets, in which case both Provision 2.A.9 and Provision 2.A.11 apply. As an example, a portfolio may have a criterion systematically applied at the investment level to hold only securities with an ESG rating of BBB or higher and have a portfolio-level target to maintain a weighted average ESG rating of AA.

Some portfolio-level ESG characteristic targets may apply to only a portion of the portfolio, such as to one asset class but not another. As long as there is a target for a portfolio-level ESG characteristic, Provision 2.A.11 applies.

Provision 2.A.11

If the INVESTMENT PRODUCT has targets for portfolio-level ESG characteristics, then the INVESTMENT MANAGER MUST disclose for each target:

a. the portfolio-level ESG characteristic that is evaluated.

Discussion

Investment managers must disclose each portfolio-level ESG characteristic for which there is a target. If the ESG characteristic is not readily understood, investment managers are encouraged to provide a description of the ESG characteristic.

Provision 2.A.11

If the INVESTMENT PRODUCT has targets for portfolio-level ESG characteristics, then the INVESTMENT MANAGER MUST disclose for each target:

b. how the portfolio-level ESG characteristic is measured.

Discussion

Investment managers must disclose how an ESG characteristic for which there is a portfolio-level target is measured, such as the calculation or methodology used to measure or quantify the ESG characteristic or the observable state that correlates with the ESG characteristic. For example, consider an investment product with a portfolio-level target for carbon intensity. The investment manager must provide information on how it measures carbon intensity.

Provision 2.A.11

If the INVESTMENT PRODUCT has targets for portfolio-level ESG characteristics, then the INVESTMENT MANAGER MUST disclose for each target:

c. the target value or range for the portfolio-level ESG characteristic.

Discussion

A portfolio-level target for an ESG characteristic may be stated as a target value, a minimum or maximum, or a range. Portfolio-level ESG characteristic targets may be set on an absolute or relative basis. As an example, a portfolio with a weighted average ESG rating target of AA has an absolute target. As another example, an investment product that aims to have a carbon footprint that is not more than 75% of the carbon footprint of its benchmark has a relative target. In either case, the investment manager must disclose the target value or target range for the portfolio-level ESG characteristic.

Provision 2.A.11

If the INVESTMENT PRODUCT has targets for portfolio-level ESG characteristics, then the INVESTMENT MANAGER MUST disclose for each target:

d. how the target portfolio-level ESG characteristic is expected to be attained.

Discussion

Investment managers must disclose the manner in which the portfolio-level ESG characteristic target is expected to be attained. When describing how the target is to be attained, an investment manager might describe the security selection process, the portfolio construction process, and whether the target is attained through direct exposure or through the use of derivatives.

Provision 2.A.11

If the INVESTMENT PRODUCT has targets for portfolio-level ESG characteristics, then the INVESTMENT MANAGER MUST disclose for each target:

e. the risks that could significantly hinder the attainment of the target portfolio-level ESG characteristic, should they occur.

Discussion

There is always a possibility that a portfolio-level ESG characteristic target will not be attained. To allow an investor to assess the likelihood that such a target will or will not be attained, the investment manager must disclose the risks that could significantly hinder the attainment of the ESG characteristic target. Investment managers need not list every risk imaginable but must disclose foreseeable risks that, were they to occur, are likely to prevent the target from being attained. As an example, consider a portfolio that seeks to maintain a weighted average ESG rating of AAA. At times, there is a risk that the weighted average ESG portfolio rating of AAA may be unattainable because of a lack of sufficient investment opportunities in securities with ESG ratings of AA and AAA that are consistent with the investment product's strategy.

Sample Disclosure for Provisions 2.A.11.a–2.A.11.e

"The Fund seeks to maintain a weighted average carbon intensity (WACI) target that is at least 50% lower than the WACI of its benchmark. Carbon intensity measures how efficiently a company uses its carbon resources to generate revenue and allows for carbon efficiency comparison among companies of different sizes.

The WACI of the Fund is the carbon intensity of the Fund's holdings aggregated according to the percentage weighting of each holding. Carbon intensity is calculated as a company's Scope 1 + Scope 2 greenhouse gas emissions in carbon dioxide equivalents normalized by USD1 million in revenue. A carbon dioxide equivalent compares the global warming potential from various greenhouse gases by converting amounts of other types of greenhouse gases to the equivalent amount of carbon dioxide with the same global warming potential.

To achieve the Fund's investment objective as well as its WACI target, the Fund invests in companies we believe have attractive valuations and lower carbon intensity relative to industry peers. The WACI target is recalculated quarterly to reflect changes in the WACI of the benchmark.

At times, the portfolio's benchmark-relative WACI target may not be attained because of natural variations in the carbon intensity of index constituents, changes made to index constituents, and lags in vendor-supplied data versus benchmark data."

Provision 2.A.11

If the INVESTMENT PRODUCT has targets for portfolio-level ESG characteristics, then the INVESTMENT MANAGER MUST disclose for each target:

f. a reference, where applicable, to any law, regulation, or third-party standard, guideline, or framework used to measure the portfolio-level ESG characteristic or set the target.

Discussion

The disclosure for a portfolio-level ESG characteristic target must reference any law, regulation, or third-party standard, guideline, or framework used to measure the portfolio-level ESG characteristic or set the target. An investment manager must also disclose any third-party standard, guideline, or framework used to determine a calculation methodology for a portfolio-level ESG characteristic or set a threshold level for a target.

Sample Disclosure

"The Fund targets a 1.5-degree Celsius warming limit consistent with the Paris Agreement goals. To meet this warming limit target, the Fund invests in fixed-income securities that are Climate Bonds Certified. These securities are compatible with a 1.5-degree Celsius warming limit as determined by the Climate Bonds Taxonomy."

Provision 2.A.12

If the INVESTMENT PRODUCT uses an ESG INDEX as a point of comparison for portfolio-level ESG characteristics, then the INVESTMENT MANAGER MUST disclose:

a. the portfolio-level ESG characteristics that are compared with the ESG INDEX.

Discussion

ESG index characteristics may be used as points of comparison for portfolio-level ESG characteristics. Provision 2.A.12.a requires an investment manager to disclose the specific ESG characteristics of the investment product that are compared with ESG characteristics of an ESG index. If the ESG characteristic is not one that is readily understood, the investment manager is encouraged to provide a description of the ESG characteristic.

Provision 2.A.12

If the INVESTMENT PRODUCT uses an ESG INDEX as a point of comparison for portfolio-level ESG characteristics, then the INVESTMENT MANAGER MUST disclose:

b. either the significant ESG characteristics of the index or, if the index is a readily recognized index, the name of the index.

Discussion

A significant ESG index characteristic is an index characteristic based on ESG issues or information that is likely to be of importance to an investor when choosing an investment product that uses the ESG index as its investment universe. Some examples of types of significant ESG characteristics of an ESG index include but are not limited to:

- specific ESG themes, such as gender diversity;
- index-level ESG statistics or metrics, such as carbon exposure metrics;

- ESG-related exclusions; and
- the use of ESG scores or ratings in constituent selection.

If the ESG index is a readily recognized index, providing the ESG index name will satisfy Provision 2.A.12.b. Each investment manager must decide for itself whether an index is readily recognized. If the investment manager is uncertain as to whether the ESG index is readily recognized, the investment manager must describe the significant ESG characteristics of the index.

Sample Disclosure for Provisions 2.A.12.a and 2.A.12.b

"The Fund measures its weighted average carbon intensity and its fossil fuel reserve emissions against those of the XYZ Global Broad Market ESG Index. Carbon intensity measures how efficiently a company uses its carbon resources to generate revenue and allows for carbon efficiency comparison among companies of different sizes. Fossil fuel reserve emissions are potential greenhouse gas emissions stored in companies' fossil fuel reserves.

The XYZ Global Broad Market ESG Index is a broad market equity index with the following significant ESG characteristics:

- constituents selected based on an ESG scoring system,
- exclusions based on certain business activities and ESG controversies, and
- index-level carbon metrics."

Provision 2.A.12

If the INVESTMENT PRODUCT uses an ESG INDEX as a point of comparison for portfolio-level ESG characteristics, then the INVESTMENT MANAGER MUST disclose:

c. how an INVESTOR can obtain information about the definitions of and calculation methodologies for the ESG characteristics of the ESG INDEX.

Discussion

Provision 2.A.12.c requires that investment managers disclose how investors can obtain information about the definitions of an ESG index's ESG characteristics and the methodologies used to calculate those ESG characteristics. This disclosure can take various forms, such as the provision of an index webpage address or an embedded link in the ESG Disclosure Statement that will lead investors to the required information.

Sample Disclosure

"Information about the XYZ Global Broad Market ESG Index is available on the website of the Index Administrator, XYZ Index Creator AG."

Provision 2.A.13

If the INVESTMENT PRODUCT has targets for portfolio-level ESG characteristics, then the INVESTMENT MANAGER MUST disclose how progress toward, or attainment of, those targets is reported to INVESTORS.

Discussion

Progress toward, or attainment of, portfolio-level ESG characteristic targets should be measured by a quantifiable metric or observable state that correlates with the ESG characteristic target. An investment manager must disclose the manner in which information on progress toward, or attainment of, the ESG characteristic targets is reported to investors—such as through quarterly emailed reports or a document on the investment manager's website. If progress toward, or attainment of, portfolio-level ESG characteristic targets is not reported to investors, the investment manager must disclose that such progress or attainment is not reported.

Sample Disclosure

"The XYZ Climate Fund reports its carbon footprint and weighted average carbon intensity in the Fund's Quarterly Investment Report. This report can be found on XYZ Asset Management's website at XYZAssetManagement.com/XYZ. Investors can also request a copy of the XYZ Climate Fund's Quarterly Investment Report by emailing us at info@XYZAssetManagement.com."

Portfolio-Level Allocation Targets

Provision 2.A.14

If the INVESTMENT PRODUCT has portfolio-level allocation targets for investments that have specific ESG characteristics, then the INVESTMENT MANAGER MUST disclose for each allocation target:

a. the specific ESG characteristics of the investments for which there is an allocation target; and

b. the allocation target value or range.

Discussion

A portfolio-level allocation target is a target to hold a specified portion of a portfolio in certain types of securities or investments with certain characteristics. Investment managers may set portfolio-level allocation targets for investments with characteristics that are based on ESG information or ESG issues, such as ESG ratings, low-carbon securities, ESG-related thematic investments, or sustainable investments. For example, a portfolio that is required to hold a minimum of 80% of its market value in securities with an ESG rating of BBB or higher has a portfolio-level allocation target.

A portfolio-level allocation target for securities with specific ESG characteristics does not imply, nor require, that each investment in the portfolio has that characteristic. If an investment product has an ESG characteristic target that every investment must meet in order to be included in the portfolio, and any investment that does not have that ESG characteristic is excluded, then the investment product has a systematically applied screening criterion and Provision 2.A.9, Screening, applies. For example, an investment product that requires 100% of its investments to have an ESG rating of BBB or higher has a criterion that is systematically applied at the investment level, thus triggering Provision 2.A.9.

An investment product can have both investment-level ESG screening criteria and portfolio-level allocation targets for investments with ESG characteristics, in which case both Provision 2.A.9 and Provision 2.A.14 apply. As an example, an investment product may exclude all securities with an ESG rating of B or lower, triggering Provision 2.A.9, while also having a portfolio-level allocation target to hold a minimum of 50% of its market value in securities with an ESG rating of A or higher, which triggers Provision 2.A.14.

Provision 2.A.14

If the INVESTMENT PRODUCT has portfolio-level allocation targets for investments that have specific ESG characteristics, then the INVESTMENT MANAGER MUST disclose for each allocation target:

a. the specific ESG characteristics of the investments for which there is an allocation target.

Discussion

For each portfolio-level allocation target, the investment manager must describe the specific ESG characteristic of the underlying investments for which there is an allocation target. If the ESG characteristic is not one that is readily understood, the investment manager is encouraged to provide a description of the ESG characteristic. Some examples of ESG characteristics for which there may be a portfolio-level allocation target include, but are not limited to, the following:

- a green bond label,
- investments deemed to be sustainable by a regulatory or third-party classification standard,
- business activities that have adverse effects on ESG issues, or
- ESG scores or ratings.

Provision 2.A.14

If the INVESTMENT PRODUCT has portfolio-level allocation targets for investments that have specific ESG characteristics, then the INVESTMENT MANAGER MUST disclose for each allocation target:

b. the allocation target value or range.

Discussion

Portfolio-level allocation targets are typically stated as a minimum, a maximum, or a range. Portfolio-level allocation targets may be fixed or relative. For example, consider an alternative energy thematic investment product that targets an 80% allocation to clean energy securities. This allocation target is an example of a fixed allocation target. Another investment product might target a weighting for companies with fossil fuel reserves that is 20% lower than the weighting of companies with fossil fuel reserves in its benchmark. This allocation target is an example of a relative allocation target. Provision 2.A.14 is not triggered based on whether a portfolio-level allocation target is fixed or relative; rather, it is triggered simply by the presence of the portfolio-level allocation target.

Sample Disclosure 1 for Provisions 2.A.14.a and 2.A.14.b

"The Fund aims to invest at least 25% of the market value of its fixed-income holdings in labeled green bonds and Certified Climate Bonds.

- *Labeled green bonds* are bonds that earmark proceeds for climate or environmental projects and have been labeled as "green" by the issuer.
- *Certified Climate Bonds* are bonds and loans that are verified to conform with the Climate Bonds Standard, a science-based standard for identifying projects and assets that are consistent with the Paris Agreement goals for a low-carbon economy. (Source: Climate Bonds Initiative)"

Sample Disclosure 2 for Provisions 2.A.14.a and 2.A.14.b

"The Fund invests a minimum of 60% of its market value in companies that have strong ESG practices as determined by our proprietary ESG scoring system. We define companies with strong ESG practices as companies that have a proprietary ESG score ranging from 8 to 10. This system scores companies on a range of ESG factors, including but not limited to the establishment of a science-based decarbonization pathway, the implementation of diversity and inclusion best practice policies, fair labor practices, business ethics principles and record of violations, and the degree of governing board independence."

Provision 2.A.15

If the INVESTMENT PRODUCT has portfolio-level allocation targets for investments that have specific ESG characteristics, then the INVESTMENT MANAGER MUST disclose how progress toward, or attainment of, those targets is reported to INVESTORS.

Discussion

Progress toward, or attainment of, portfolio-level allocation targets should be measured by a quantifiable metric or observable state that correlates with the allocation target. An investment manager must disclose the manner in which information on progress toward, or attainment of, the ESG characteristic targets is reported to investors—such as through quarterly emailed reports or a document on the investment manager's website.

Sample Disclosure

"The Fund's allocation to labeled green bonds and Certified Climate Bonds is reported in Quarterly Fund Reports. Quarterly Fund Reports are distributed to investors via email and are also available on the Fund's website at www.XYZClimateFund.com/QuarterlyReports."

Stewardship Activities

Provision 2.A.16

The INVESTMENT MANAGER MUST disclose how an INVESTOR can obtain a complete and current copy of all of the policies that govern the INVESTMENT PRODUCT'S STEWARDSHIP ACTIVITIES.

Discussion

Provision 2.A.16 requires investment managers to disclose how investors can obtain a complete and current copy of all stewardship policies that apply to the investment product, regardless of whether a stewardship policy is specific to the investment product or applies to all of the investment manager's investment products. This disclosure can take various forms, such as the provision of a webpage address or an embedded link within the ESG Disclosure Statement to the stewardship policies that apply to the investment product.

Sample Disclosure

"To receive a copy of Smoke Capital's stewardship policy, please email your request to: clientservices@smokecapital.com."

Provision 2.A.17

If ESG issues are typically considered when undertaking STEWARDSHIP ACTIVITIES, the INVESTMENT MANAGER MUST disclose:

a. the types of STEWARDSHIP ACTIVITIES typically undertaken for the INVESTMENT PRODUCT, differentiated by type of investment where necessary.

Discussion

Provision 2.A.17.a requires that investment managers disclose the types of stewardship activities that are typically undertaken for the investment product. An investment manager need not disclose every stewardship activity undertaken; only those activities that are typically undertaken must be disclosed. Because not all types of stewardship activities are applicable to every type of investment—for example, proxy voting is conducted for equity investments but not for fixed-income investments—investment managers must differentiate stewardship activities by type of investment where necessary.

Provision 2.A.17

If ESG issues are typically considered when undertaking STEWARDSHIP ACTIVITIES, the INVESTMENT MANAGER MUST disclose:

b. the ESG issues typically considered when undertaking those STEWARDSHIP ACTIVITIES.

Discussion

Regardless of whether the decision to consider ESG issues when undertaking stewardship activities is based on an investment product–level stewardship policy or a firm-wide stewardship policy, Provision 2.A.17.b applies as long as the investment manager considers ESG issues when undertaking stewardship activities for the investments held by the investment product. An investment manager need not list every ESG issue that might be considered in its stewardship activities; only those ESG issues that are typically considered must be disclosed. For example, one investment manager may routinely consider climate change issues when undertaking its stewardship activities, whereas another investment manager may routinely consider any ESG issues it believes pose a financially material risk to an investee company.

Provision 2.A.17

If ESG issues are typically considered when undertaking STEWARDSHIP ACTIVITIES, the INVESTMENT MANAGER MUST disclose:

c. how those STEWARDSHIP ACTIVITIES and ESG issues are relevant to the INVESTMENT PRODUCT'S objectives and investment process.

Discussion

Provision 2.A.17.c requires an investment manager to disclose how the ESG issues that are typically considered during typical stewardship activities for the investment product are relevant to the investment product's objectives and investment process. For example, an investment manager may vote proxies and engage management in order to encourage an investee company to reduce its climate change risks because the investment manager believes reducing these risks can help lower investment risk, thus contributing to achieving the investment product's financial objective. As another example, an investment manager may engage with investee companies in order to obtain ESG information that can be used in its research and analysis process.

Sample Disclosure for Provisions 2.A.17.a–2.A.17.c

"Our stewardship activities for the Global Balanced Fund include proxy voting, engagement, and advocacy. We vote proxies for all equities held in our portfolio and engage with certain equity and fixed-income issuers. Engagement is conducted in accordance with the Fund's Engagement Policy and includes email correspondence, meetings with company management, and collaborative shareholder dialogues with issuers. Advocacy efforts include providing comment letters to regulators. We align our proxy voting decisions with our engagement efforts.

Our stewardship activities prioritize issues related to climate risk, which we believe poses a systemic global financial risk, and corporate governance. Specifically, with respect to corporate governance, we prioritize the following issues: shareholder rights, board and committee structure and degree of independence, directors' skills and experience, transparency and accountability, and executive remuneration. We believe these corporate governance issues affect the long-term financial performance of the companies we own.

Information on our proxy voting, engagement, and advocacy activities can be found in our Annual Stewardship Reports."

Provision 2.A.17

If ESG issues are typically considered when undertaking STEWARDSHIP ACTIVITIES, the INVESTMENT MANAGER MUST disclose:

d. the processes and systems that support the STEWARDSHIP ACTIVITIES undertaken for the INVESTMENT PRODUCT.

Discussion

Provision 2.A.17.d requires an investment manager to provide information that enables investors to understand how an investment product's stewardship activities are implemented. Examples of processes and systems that support an investment product's stewardship activities include but are not limited to the steps an investment manager takes to implement stewardship activities, such as the proxy voting process; the software, platforms, or methods used to monitor and assess engagement efforts and outcomes; and the organizational roles or committees that carry out the stewardship activities. An investment manager is not required to provide names of the software, platforms, or vendors it uses, but an investment manager may provide this information if it so chooses. Because processes and systems can differ for the various types of stewardship activities, investment managers must describe processes and systems for each type of stewardship activity undertaken.

Sample Disclosure 1

"Proxies are voted for all of the Fund's equity holdings. Records of all proxy votes cast or abstained are maintained in our stewardship management system. Engagement activities include attending in-person and virtual meetings and corresponding with investee companies. The Fund's engagement officer flags companies and issues for engagement. Once an engagement effort is initiated, all written communications, meeting records, and targeted engagement outcomes are logged in the stewardship management system. On a quarterly basis, the Fund's engagement officer reviews progress made toward the targeted outcomes and determines next steps in accordance with the Fund's Engagement Policy."

Sample Disclosure 2

"We subscribe to a third-party service that issues alerts when a company we own has violated international principles, standards, or norms related to the environment, human rights, or business ethics. For each company and each issue flagged for engagement, we maintain a database of engagement records. The database records include copies of written communications and records of meeting dates, attendees, locations, discussion topics, and desired outcomes. Alerts are set up in our internal engagement tracking system for our engagement team to review each engagement effort annually against engagement goals. Progress toward goals is tracked internally and via our third-party service provider's monitoring service. We also use the service provider's recordkeeping system to maintain a log of all proxy votes cast, searchable by date and topic."

Provision 2.A.18

The INVESTMENT MANAGER MUST disclose how STEWARDSHIP ACTIVITIES for the INVESTMENT PRODUCT are reported to INVESTORS.

Discussion

An investment manager is required to disclose the manner in which it reports its stewardship activities to investors—such as through quarterly emailed reports or a document on the investment manager's website. If stewardship activities are not reported to investors, the investment manager must disclose that stewardship activities are not reported to investors.

Sample Disclosure

"Information regarding the stewardship activities for this investment product is included in the XYZ Asset Management Annual Stewardship Report. This report can be found on XYZ Asset Management's website at XYZAssetManagement.com/stewardship. Investors can also request a copy of the Annual Stewardship Report by emailing clientsupport@xyzassetmanagement.com or writing to XYZ Asset Management Company, ATTN: Compliance Department, 1234 Alpha Summit Lane, Suite 1111, New York, NY 10005."

Environmental and Social Impact Objectives

Provision 2.A.19

If investments are made with the intention to generate positive, measurable SOCIAL and ENVIRONMENTAL impact alongside a financial return, then the INVESTMENT MANAGER MUST disclose:

a. the impact objectives in measurable or observable terms;
b. the stakeholders who will benefit from the attainment of the impact objectives;
c. the time horizon over which the impact objectives are expected to be attained;
d. how the impact objectives are related to other objectives that the INVESTMENT PRODUCT has and how the pursuit of the impact objectives could result in trade-offs with those other objectives;
e. how the attainment of the impact objectives will contribute to third-party sustainable development goals, if there is a stated intention to do so;
f. the proportion of the portfolio committed to generating SOCIAL and ENVIRONMENTAL impact;
g. how the impact objectives are expected to be attained;
h. the risks that could significantly hinder the attainment of the impact objectives, should they occur;
i. how progress toward, or attainment of, the impact objectives is measured, monitored, and evaluated;
j. how progress toward the attainment of the impact objectives is reported to INVESTORS; and
k. the process for assessing, addressing, monitoring, and managing potential negative SOCIAL and ENVIRONMENTAL impacts that may occur in the course of attaining the impact objectives.

Discussion

If an investment product has only a single impact objective, the information required by Provision 2.A.19 needs to be disclosed only once. If an investment product has multiple impact objectives, the information required by Provision 2.A.19 must be disclosed for each impact objective. If an investment product has many diverse investments and the investment manager is unable to provide meaningful, specific information for an impact objective as required by Provision 2.A.19, the investment manager must not state in the investment product's ESG Disclosure Statement that the investment product has that impact objective. In this case, the investment manager is encouraged to review Provision 2.A.11, Portfolio-Level ESG

Characteristics, and Provision 2.A.14, Portfolio-Level Allocation Targets, to determine if the investment product should be described as having a portfolio-level ESG characteristic target or a portfolio-level allocation target.

Provision 2.A.19

If investments are made with the intention to generate positive, measurable SOCIAL and ENVIRONMENTAL impact alongside a financial return, then the INVESTMENT MANAGER MUST disclose:

a. the impact objectives in measurable or observable terms.

Discussion

Investment products that have an impact objective allow investors to contribute to that impact objective through the investment of their capital. If an investment manager states that an investment product has one or more impact objectives, Provision 2.A.19.a requires the investment manager to disclose the impact objectives in measurable or observable terms—that is, the investment manager must clearly describe the specific outcome the investment product intends to attain when seeking to make an impact on an environmental or social issue.

Some impact objectives are best stated in terms of qualitative or quantitative characteristics of the desired end state—for instance, "municipal drinking water in the XYZ region will conform to World Health Organization drinking water guidelines" or the "conservation of 500,000 acres of sustainable timberland." Other impact objectives are best described in terms of a tangible or observable change that is expected to take place—for instance, "a water treatment facility will be built to serve the XYZ region." In each of these examples, the impact objective is measurable or observable.

An investment manager must not state that the investment product has an impact objective if the impact objective is not explicitly expressed in the documents that govern the investment product. Impact objectives may be included in an ESG Disclosure Statement only when the impact objective has been established prior to the occurrence of the impact and the investment manager has a process in place to attain the impact objective. An investment manager must not add an impact objective to an ESG Disclosure Statement after an impact has occurred and then claim that the investment product's investments resulted in that impact. An investment manager also must not claim in an ESG Disclosure Statement that the investment product has an objective to attain an impact outcome that it anticipates will result indirectly from the investment product's investments; "collateral" impact outcomes that were not attained intentionally must not be claimed as impact objectives.

Provision 2.A.19.a requires only a description of the impact objective, but investment managers are encouraged to provide additional information about the current state of the environmental or social issues relevant to the impact objective. This information provides investors with context to understand the magnitude of the impact sought and the degree to which stakeholders will benefit if the impact objective is achieved.

Sample Disclosure 1

"The BCD Biodiversity Fund was created to help prevent biodiversity loss in critical habitats and ecosystems in South America. These habitats promote economic stability and growth, contribute to sustainable food sources and income for area inhabitants, and combat climate change. Biodiversity loss occurs for a number of reasons, including extensive deforestation and exploitive land management practices. The Fund provides a vehicle for investors to address these environmental challenges while earning a return on investment.

Preservation of South American biodiversity and forests has important implications for society at large, including but not limited to climate change mitigation from preventing the release of greenhouse gas emissions; a reduction in food insecurity from implementing sustainable agricultural practices; and the preservation of a rich source of natural resources that have yielded important medicinal solutions. The Fund has the following impact performance goals:

IRIS Metric	Performance Goal
Forest Management Plan—OI2622	200,000 hectares sustainably managed
Land Directly Controlled: Sustainably Managed—OI6912"	300,000 hectares sustainably managed

Sample Disclosure 2

"The Fund aims to contribute to the mitigation of global warming by investing in companies with greenhouse gas emissions that exceed limits consistent with the Paris Agreement goals and using active and collaborative engagement to bring about a reduction in company emissions in line with a 1.5-degree Celsius warming scenario."

Provision 2.A.19

If investments are made with the intention to generate positive, measurable SOCIAL and ENVIRONMENTAL impact alongside a financial return, then the INVESTMENT MANAGER MUST disclose:

b. the stakeholders who will benefit from the attainment of the impact objectives.

Discussion

Stakeholders who will benefit from the attainment of the impact objectives are those who are ultimately helped through the actions of the investee entities. Stakeholders do not include the investment product's investors, the investment manager that offers the investment product, the managers of the investee entities, or other investors of investee entities. Stakeholders are third parties that are affected by the decisions of investment managers and investee entities but are not formally part of the investment decision-making process. Stakeholders include but are not limited to members of a specific group or community, employees of an investee entity, customers of an investee entity, suppliers of an investee entity, animals, marine life, and environmental systems. If a stakeholder is a group of people, the stakeholder description must include information about that group's characteristics. If a stakeholder is an animal or marine life population, the stakeholder description must include information about the characteristics of the animal or marine life population. If a stakeholder is an environmental system, the stakeholder description must include information about the type of environmental system and the primary geographical area that will benefit from the intended outcome.

Sample Disclosure 1

"The Fund's investments in women's healthcare clinics in Chad and South Sudan are intended to improve healthcare access and quality for an estimated 150,000 women."

Sample Disclosure 2

"Global warming will affect many aspects of life in South America, including human life, life on land, and life below water. The Fund aims to contribute to climate change mitigation, thus helping to protect the Amazon rainforest ecosystem."

Provision 2.A.19

If investments are made with the intention to generate positive, measurable SOCIAL and ENVIRONMENTAL impact alongside a financial return, then the INVESTMENT MANAGER MUST disclose:

c. the time horizon over which the impact objectives are expected to be attained.

Discussion

The investment manager must disclose the time horizon over which the impact objectives are expected to be attained. In some cases, an impact objective may be expected to be attained by a specific target date. For example, an investment product might consist of a partnership formed solely to fund a specific infrastructure project that has an estimated completion date. As another example, the time horizon may span a period, such as "three to five years." In another instance, an investment product may have multiple impact objectives expected to be attained over the investment product's life span. In these instances, the impact objectives are expected to be attained on different dates or over different periods. In all cases, the expected time horizon for each impact objective must be disclosed.

Sample Disclosure 1

"The River Fund's capital will be invested in private debt investments. The Fund's objective is projected to be achieved over the 10-year expected life of the Fund as projects are completed and loans are repaid."

Sample Disclosure 2

"The objectives of the QRS Decarbonization Engagement Fund are to (1) achieve an equity market rate of return over the long term and (2) actively engage with portfolio companies to reduce their greenhouse gas emissions (GHG) to a level consistent with a 1.5-degree Celsius warming limit, by 2030, in alignment with global GHG emission reduction targets set by the Paris Agreement. Specific impact time horizons are determined for each portfolio company prior to investing."

Provision 2.A.19

If investments are made with the intention to generate positive, measurable SOCIAL and ENVIRONMENTAL impact alongside a financial return, then the INVESTMENT MANAGER MUST disclose:

d. how the impact objectives are related to other objectives that the INVESTMENT PRODUCT has and how the pursuit of the impact objectives could result in trade-offs with those other objectives.

Discussion

When an investment product has two or more objectives that are to be simultaneously attained, the objectives may be in conflict, complementary, or unrelated. The relationship between any two or more objectives may vary in nature and degree under different circumstances. The relationship could be in conflict in some ways and complementary in other ways at the same time. For example, consider an investment product that has a financial objective to "meet or exceed the total return of the ABC benchmark" and an impact objective to "reduce the impact of climate change on agriculture yields in the XYZ region." The investment manager will seek investments that simultaneously meet both objectives. Temporary circumstances, however, such as certain market conditions, may force the investment manager to prioritize one objective over the other.

Consider another investment product that has a financial objective to "preserve capital and earn income by providing long-term loans for the development of schools in the XYZ region" and an impact objective to "increase the literacy rate of school-age children in the XYZ region." At first, it may seem that the two objectives are completely complementary. With respect to outcomes, however, trade-offs may exist. Perhaps more schools could be built if the investment product offered loans at below-market interest rates. Doing so would advance the attainment of the impact objective but hinder the achievement of the financial objective.

Provision 2.A.19.d requires the investment manager to disclose how an investment product's impact objective is related to its financial or other impact objectives and the trade-offs that could result from the pursuit of the impact objective. Provision 2.A.19.d does not intend to imply that financial objectives and impact objectives are always in conflict and cannot be complementary or unrelated. For investors to make informed decisions, however, they must understand how the impact objectives relate to the investment product's other objectives, as well as potential trade-offs that could result from pursuing the impact objectives.

Sample Disclosure 1

"The BCD Biodiversity Fund seeks to generate a target internal rate of return (IRR) and meet key performance indicators (KPIs) for its environmental impact objectives over the Fund's expected 10-year life. We believe sustainable forestry and land management practices will be key drivers of value creation for the Fund's investments and that attainment of the impact performance goals will help the Fund achieve its target IRR.

Prior to making an investment, BCD assesses potential investee companies first for the likelihood of achieving predetermined KPIs related to biodiversity loss mitigation and second for the ability to contribute to achieving the target IRR over the life of the Fund. To meet the Fund's impact objectives, it may be necessary at times for the Fund to prioritize investments with a greater potential for impact relative to financial performance. The Fund will engage in these trade-offs while striving to achieve an IRR within the stated target range."

Sample Disclosure 2

"Security selection begins with ranking companies in the Fund's universe within their industries according to their carbon intensity and then analyzing the feasibility of using engagement to facilitate a meaningful reduction in GHG emissions. Financial analysis screens are applied to arrive at a set of securities that has the potential to meet both the Fund's financial and impact objectives. It may be necessary at times to invest in securities that will help the Fund meet its financial objective but that may not meet the Fund's impact objective. These securities will be limited to 20% of the Fund's market value."

Provision 2.A.19

If investments are made with the intention to generate positive, measurable SOCIAL and ENVIRONMENTAL impact alongside a financial return, then the INVESTMENT MANAGER MUST disclose:

e. how the attainment of the impact objectives will contribute to third-party sustainable development goals, if there is a stated intention to do so.

Discussion

If an investment manager states that an investment product's impact objectives will contribute to one or more third-party sustainable development goals, the investment manager must explain how attaining the impact objectives contributes to each sustainable development goal. Investment managers are encouraged to provide additional information about any sustainable development goal that serves as an impact objective and the corresponding government or organization that set the sustainable development goal.

Alignment with third-party sustainable development goals alone does not constitute an impact objective. For an investment manager to state that an investment product has an impact objective related to a third-party sustainable development goal, there must be an ex ante intention to contribute to the stated third-party sustainable development goal.

Sample Disclosure 1

"By providing direct loans that finance safe, durable, and affordable housing in underserved communities, this strategy aims to contribute to the United Nations Sustainable Development Goal (SDG) 11, Sustainable Cities and Communities. SDG 11 seeks to make cities and human settlements inclusive, safe, resilient, and sustainable."

Sample Disclosure 2

"Through its impact investments, the Fund seeks to contribute to UN Sustainable Development Goal 15: *Protect, restore and promote sustainable use of terrestrial ecosystems, sustainably manage forests, combat desertification, and halt and reverse land degradation and halt biodiversity loss.* South America is home to some of the most diverse ecosystems on the planet, and also some of the most endangered. These habitats promote economic stability and growth, contribute to sustainable food sources and income for area inhabitants, and combat climate change. Biodiversity

 |

loss occurs for a number of reasons, including extensive deforestation and exploitive land management practices. The Fund provides a vehicle for investors to address these environmental challenges by investing in companies that provide solutions for protecting and restoring fragile ecosystems and habitats through sustainable forestry and land management practices."

Provision 2.A.19

If investments are made with the intention to generate positive, measurable SOCIAL and ENVIRONMENTAL impact alongside a financial return, then the INVESTMENT MANAGER MUST disclose:

f. the proportion of the portfolio committed to generating SOCIAL and ENVIRONMENTAL impact.

Discussion

An impact objective might not be established for every investment in the portfolio or considered as part of every investment decision. An impact objective may apply to only certain types of investments in a portfolio or to only a certain portion of the portfolio. For example, a private debt fund may allocate a certain portion of its investments to achieving an impact objective while allocating the remainder to non-impact investments. Provision 2.A.19.f requires an investment manager to disclose the proportion of the portfolio, whether it is the entire portfolio or some portion of the portfolio, that is committed to generating social and environmental impact. If the impact objective does not apply to all investments, the investment manager must describe the investments, in terms of their characteristics or in terms of the portion of the portfolio, to which the impact objective applies.

Sample Disclosure 1

"The Biodiversity Fund intends to invest the Fund's £125M of committed capital in direct equity and debt in enterprises that provide solutions to protect and restore fragile ecosystems and habitats through sustainable forestry and land management practices."

Sample Disclosure 2

"The Fund invests a minimum of 80% of its capital in the green bonds of issuers that adhere to the Green Bond Principles and that manage, report on, and assess the impact of the bonds' proceeds. The Fund also invests in US Treasuries, government agency securities, and money market instruments for the purposes of liquidity and interest rate management; these securities are not intended to be impact investments."

Provision 2.A.19

If investments are made with the intention to generate positive, measurable SOCIAL and ENVIRONMENTAL impact alongside a financial return, then the INVESTMENT MANAGER MUST disclose:

g. how the impact objectives are expected to be attained.

Discussion

When disclosing how the investment product's impact objectives are expected to be attained through the investment product's investments, the investment manager must explain how the funding of certain projects or enterprises, or types of projects or enterprises, is expected to result in the desired outcomes. When applicable, the investment manager may choose to describe how an impact objective is advanced through pre-investment negotiations with potential investee companies regarding the conditions for investment, including but not limited to type of investment, size of investment, debt covenants, seats on the board of directors, adherence to standards, and requirements for certain policies, procedures, and reporting.

In addition to the investment product's investments, the investment manager's stewardship activities may also contribute to the attainment of the impact objectives. When disclosing how the investment product's impact objectives are expected to be attained through stewardship activities, the investment manager must include an explanation of how the specific stewardship activities are expected to result in the impact objectives. In particular, the investment manager may want to consider the levers of influence available to it and how such levers will be used, including but not limited to the following:

- the legal rights available to the financiers and owners of the projects or enterprises in which the investment product invests, and the extent to which the investment manager expects to exercise those rights;
- the level of control or influence that the investment manager exerts over the project or enterprise, via the investment product and in aggregate;
- the extent to which the investment manager expects to engage with the project manager or enterprise;
- the extent to which the investment manager expects to collaborate with other investors and organizations; and
- the extent to which the investment manager expects to advocate for changes that would support the desired outcomes.

If an investment manager is relying on stewardship activities to attain an impact objective, and a reasonable possibility exists that the investment manager will not have enough influence through its stewardship activities to attain that impact objective, Provision 2.A.19.h requires that this possibility be described as a risk that could significantly hinder the attainment of the impact objective. If it is probable that the investment manager's stewardship activities will not result in the attainment of an impact objective, the investment manager should not claim the investment product has that impact objective.

Investing in publicly traded equity securities without an ex ante intention to use engagement or other stewardship activities to attain a specific impact objective is unlikely to result in a positive, measurable, or observable contribution to an environmental or social issue.

Sample Disclosure 1

"The Fund aims to achieve its objective of creating a tangible, positive, societal impact by providing direct, flexible loans that finance safe, affordable, quality housing in underserved communities. Prior to originating a loan, we assess the expected impact of each project, including the impact the project will have on the community, such as the number of housing units built or preserved and the number of people potentially housed."

Sample Disclosure 2

"The Fund seeks to invest its capital in enterprises that provide sustainable solutions for forestry products, soft commodity production, and smallholder agricultural practices. As a supplier of capital to companies that may be otherwise unable to obtain funding, the Fund contributes to the mitigation of biodiversity loss in South America."

Provision 2.A.19

If investments are made with the intention to generate positive, measurable SOCIAL and ENVIRONMENTAL impact alongside a financial return, then the INVESTMENT MANAGER MUST disclose:

h. the risks that could significantly hinder the attainment of the impact objectives, should they occur.

Discussion

There is always a possibility that an impact objective will not be attained. To allow an investor to assess the likelihood of whether an impact objective will or will not be attained, the investment manager must disclose the risks that could significantly hinder the attainment of the impact objective. Investment managers need not list every possible risk imaginable but must disclose foreseeable risks that, were they to occur, are likely to prevent the impact objective from being attained.

Sample Disclosure 1

"Several risks may hinder the achievement of the Fund's impact objectives. There is a risk that one or more of the sustainable forest management or technological solutions used by enterprises in which the Fund invests may prove ineffective. The Fund may invest in start-up ventures; there is a risk that one or more new ventures may exhaust their supply of capital before one or more of the Fund's impact objectives are achieved. There is a risk that natural disasters may affect the output of certain investee companies. There is a risk that political interference may hinder the attainment of one or more impact objectives. There is a risk that the Fund may be unable to identify a sufficient number of enterprises and projects in which to invest in order to meet its impact objectives."

Sample Disclosure 2

"There is a risk that the Fund's engagement efforts will not achieve the engagement goals related to the greenhouse gas emissions reduction target set for a company. A company may choose not to respond to engagement efforts, or the company may experience a change in economic circumstances or a change in management that affects its ability or willingness to address emissions reductions. In addition, there is a risk that an error was made in our emissions estimates and that the greenhouse gas emissions target that we set for a company or companies is not feasible."

Provision 2.A.19

If investments are made with the intention to generate positive, measurable SOCIAL and ENVIRONMENTAL impact alongside a financial return, then the INVESTMENT MANAGER MUST disclose:

i. how progress toward, or attainment of, the impact objectives is measured, monitored, and evaluated.

Discussion

Investment managers must disclose the manner in which the progress and attainment of an investment product's impact objectives are measured, monitored, and evaluated. If progress toward, or attainment of, an investment product's impact objectives is measured, monitored, and evaluated using quantifiable metrics or observable states that differ from the quantifiable metrics or observable states that were used to establish the stated impact objectives, the investment manager must disclose the difference in impact assessment methodologies. To measure, monitor, and evaluate impact, investment managers are encouraged to use impact assessment methodologies developed by leading organizations that promote impact investing.

Sample Disclosure 1

"The Fund uses IRIS metrics to establish impact performance goals for investments and measure biodiversity impact outcomes. Progress toward these outcomes is measured and evaluated annually against the impact performance goals established by the IRIS metrics. If an investee company or financed project fails to achieve measurable progress as determined by annual performance goals established prior to investment, our Sustainability Team will consult with management to establish a plan of corrective action."

Sample Disclosure 2

"Both interim and long-term engagement goals may be set for a company, including but not limited to the following:

- Begin reporting on Scope 1 and Scope 2 emissions.
- Achieve a target greenhouse gas (GHG) emissions level.
- Achieve a target carbon intensity measure.
- Link executive compensation to achievement of the GHG emissions goal.

Achievement of an engagement goal is typically expected to be attained over several years. Progress toward an emissions target may be measured through the achievement of interim goals or by GHG emissions levels on a glidepath toward a targeted emissions level. Our Stewardship Team meets quarterly to review company progress and engagement responses. If the Stewardship Team determines that a company is making insufficient progress toward an impact metric, engagement is escalated according to the Fund's Engagement Policy."

Provision 2.A.19

If investments are made with the intention to generate positive, measurable SOCIAL and ENVIRONMENTAL impact alongside a financial return, then the INVESTMENT MANAGER MUST disclose:

j. how progress toward the attainment of the impact objectives is reported to INVESTORS.

Discussion

An investment manager is required to disclose the manner in which it reports information on progress toward an investment product's impact objectives to investors—such as through quarterly emailed reports or a document on the investment manager's website.

Sample Disclosure 1

"Progress on the Fund's impact objectives is measured by Key Performance Indicators at both the Fund and investee company level and is reported annually. Investors may access all Fund reports through the secure client portal on our website 90 days past quarter end."

Sample Disclosure 2

"Annual Engagement Impact Reports are available to investors on the Fund's website. Annual Engagement Impact Reports contain information on companies engaged with during the previous calendar year and the method of engagement, issues engaged on, progress toward greenhouse gas emissions targets and engagement goals, outlook for future engagement efforts, and tons of greenhouse gas emissions avoided per USD100 million at the Fund level."

Provision 2.A.19

If investments are made with the intention to generate positive, measurable SOCIAL and ENVIRONMENTAL impact alongside a financial return, then the INVESTMENT MANAGER MUST disclose:

k. the process for assessing, addressing, monitoring, and managing potential negative SOCIAL and ENVIRONMENTAL impacts that may occur in the course of attaining the impact objectives.

Discussion

In the course of attaining an impact objective, it is possible that an investment product's investments may cause, or contribute to, negative social or environmental impacts. Investment managers are therefore required to disclose the steps they take to assess, address, monitor, and manage any negative social or environmental impacts that the investment product's investments or the investments' underlying activities cause, or may cause. For example, an investment manager might conduct an assessment to identify and anticipate certain negative environmental impacts, take action to limit or mitigate those negative impacts, and then monitor the environmental effects on an ongoing basis. Investment managers must disclose their process for assessing, addressing, monitoring, and managing potential negative social and environmental impacts not only for those issues that are relevant to the impact objectives, but for all social and environmental issues relevant to the investment product's stakeholders and the social or environmental systems affected by the investment product's investments or underlying investment activities.

Sample Disclosure 1

"The Fund's Sustainability Team monitors investee company impacts on biodiversity, water, waste, and human rights to ensure its portfolio companies' greenhouse gas emissions targets are not attained through a negative impact on other key ESG issues. There is a risk that a company in which the Fund invests subsequently generates an adverse social or environmental impact or event. In these instances, the Fund's Sustainability Team, in conjunction with the Fund's portfolio managers, determines whether to sell the security or whether to engage with the company in an attempt to mitigate the adverse consequences."

Sample Disclosure 2

"Before an investment in an enterprise or project can be made, the BCD due diligence process ensures the investment conforms to our Responsible Investment Policy by avoiding investments in enterprises or projects that:

- violate the United Nations Global Compact principles,
- unlawfully infringe on the ownership or claimant rights of an indigenous people as set forth by the United Nations Declaration on the Rights of Indigenous Peoples, or
- violate sustainable agricultural and forest management processes as specified in contractual shareholder agreements and debt covenants.

Adherence to this Responsible Investment Policy is monitored as part of our quarterly review of portfolio holdings. We conduct ad hoc meetings with, and visits to, underlying companies and projects in order to assess and monitor the level and quality of impact being generated and the adherence to our Responsible Investment Policy. If, during our monitoring and review process, we identify negative impact concerns, as specified by our Responsible Investment Policy, the Sustainability Team will engage with management to identify corrective actions. If such efforts prove unsuccessful, we will evaluate the feasibility of selling the enterprise or loan in the secondary market given the estimated value of the investment and the secondary market conditions."

B. Investment Product ESG Disclosures—Recommendations

[None]

3. ESG TERMINOLOGY

A. ESG Terminology—Requirements

[None]

B. ESG Terminology—Recommendations

ESG Integration

References

> "**ESG integration:** The inclusion of ESG considerations within financial analysis and investment decisions. This may be done in various ways, tailored to the investment style and approach of the fund manager."
>
> —CFA Institute, "Certificate in ESG Investing: Official Training Manual," 3rd Edition, 2021

> "**ESG integration:** The process of including ESG factors in investment analysis and decisions to better manage risks and improve returns. It is often used in combination with screening and thematic investing."
>
> —PRI, "Reporting Framework Glossary," 2021

> "**ESG integration:** The systematic and explicit inclusion by investment managers of environmental, social and governance factors into financial analysis."
>
> —Global Sustainable Investment Alliance (GSIA), "Global Sustainable Investment Review 2020," 2020

Provision 3.B.1

The INVESTMENT MANAGER SHOULD use the term "ESG integration" in a manner consistent with the previously referenced definitions.

Discussion

Provision 2.A.7 requires that if financially material ESG information is systematically considered in investment decisions for an investment product, then the investment manager must include certain disclosures in the ESG Disclosure Statement for that investment product. The process of systematically considering financially material ESG information in investment decisions is often referred to as ESG integration. The purpose of ESG integration is to reduce the financial risks or enhance the financial returns of an investment or an investment product. It is recommended that if investment managers use the term "ESG integration" in an ESG Disclosure Statement, they do so in a manner consistent with the previously referenced definitions.

Investment managers should not use the term "ESG integration" to describe the investment processes defined under "Screening" in the following section. Investment managers also should not use the term "ESG integration" to refer to attaining portfolio-level ESG characteristics or allocation targets for investments with ESG characteristics. In some instances, the investment manager may want to consider if the terms "thematic," "sustainable," or "sustainability-themed investing," as defined later, may best describe the investment product's investments.

Provision 3.B.2

The INVESTMENT MANAGER SHOULD provide a definition for the term "ESG integration" the first time the term appears in an ESG DISCLOSURE STATEMENT.

Discussion

The investment manager is encouraged to use one of the definitions previously referenced or a definition provided by an established standard setter or industry body. An investment manager may also choose to provide its own definition, in which case the definition should be consistent with the previously referenced definitions.

Sample Disclosure for Provisions 3.B.1 and 3.B.2

"The European Equity Strategy uses ESG integration, which is defined as the process of including ESG factors in investment analysis and decisions to better manage risks and improve returns. (Source: PRI)"

Screening

References

Screening—General

"**Screening:** The application of filters to lists of potential securities, issuers, investments or sectors to rule investments in or out based on an investor's preferences, such as ethics and values, and/or investment metrics, such as risk assessments. Screening covers screening conducted under a manager's policy and client-directed screening."

—PRI, "Reporting Framework Glossary," 2021

Screening/Exclusion—Negative screening, ethical screening, faith-based screening

"**Ethical and faith-based investment:** Ethical (also known as values-driven) and faith-based investment refers to investing in line with certain principles, usually using negative screening to avoid investing in companies whose products and services are deemed morally objectionable by the investor or certain religions, international declarations, conventions, or voluntary agreements."

—CFA Institute, "Certificate in ESG Investing: Official Training Manual," 3rd Edition, 2021

"**Negative screening/exclusions/negative exclusionary screens:** Excluding certain sectors, companies or projects for their poor ESG performance relative to industry peers or based on specific ESG criteria (e.g., avoiding particular products, services or business practices)."

—PRI, "Reporting Framework Glossary," 2021

"**Negative/exclusionary screening:** The exclusion from a fund or portfolio of certain sectors, companies, countries or other issuers based on activities considered not investable. Exclusion criteria (based on norms and values) can refer, for example, to product categories (e.g., weapons, tobacco), company practices (e.g., animal testing, violation of human rights, corruption) or controversies."

—GSIA, "Global Sustainable Investment Review 2020," 2020

Screening—Norms-based

"**Norms-based screening:** Screening investments against minimum standards of business practice based on international norms. Widely recognized frameworks for minimum standards of business practice include UN treaties, Security Council sanctions, UN Global Compact, Universal Declaration of Human Rights and OECD [Organisation for Economic Co-operation and Development] guidelines."

—PRI, "Reporting Framework Glossary," 2021

"**Norms-based screening:** Screening of investments against minimum standards of business or issuer practice based on international norms such as those issued by the UN, ILO [International Labour Organization], OECD and NGOs [non-governmental organizations] (e.g., Transparency International)."

—GSIA, "Global Sustainable Investment Review 2020," 2020

Screening—Positive screening, best-in-class screening

"**Best-in-class investment:** Best-in-class investment involves selecting only the companies that overcome a defined ranking hurdle, established using ESG criteria within each sector or industry."

—CFA Institute, "Certificate in ESG Investing: Official Training Manual," 3rd Edition, 2021

"**Positive/best-in-class screening:** Investing in sectors, companies or projects selected for their positive ESG performance relative to industry peers."

—PRI, "Reporting Framework Glossary," 2021

"**Best-in-class/positive screening**: Investment in sectors, companies or projects selected for positive ESG performance relative to industry peers, and that achieve a rating above a defined threshold."

—GSIA, "Global Sustainable Investment Review 2020," 2020

Provision 3.B.3

The INVESTMENT MANAGER SHOULD provide a definition for the term "screening" (including variants that refer to a specific type of screening) the first time the term appears in an ESG DISCLOSURE STATEMENT.

Discussion

The investment manager is encouraged to use one of the definitions previously referenced for specific types of screening, such as positive or best-in-class screening, or a definition provided by an established standard setter or industry body. An investment manager may also choose to provide its own definition, in which case the definition should be consistent with the previously referenced definitions.

Sample Disclosure

"The ABC Strategy uses norms-based screening, defined by the PRI as screening investments against minimum standards of business practice based on international norms. The ABC Strategy excludes companies that are deemed to be in violation of OECD guidelines."

Thematic and Sustainability Themed Investing

References

> "**Thematic investment:** Thematic investment refers to selecting companies that fall under a sustainability-related theme, such as clean-tech, sustainable agriculture, healthcare, or climate change mitigation."
>
> —CFA Institute, "Certificate in ESG Investing: Official Training Manual," 3rd Edition, 2021

> "**Thematic investing:** The identification and allocation of capital to themes or assets related to certain environmental or social outcomes, such as clean energy, energy efficiency, or sustainable agriculture."
>
> —PRI, "Reporting Framework Glossary," 2021

> "**Sustainability Themed/Thematic Investing:** Investing in themes or assets specifically contributing to sustainable solutions—environmental and social (e.g., sustainable agriculture, green buildings, lower carbon tilted portfolio, gender equity, diversity)."
>
> —GSIA, "Global Sustainable Investment Review 2020," 2020

> "**Sustainable investment:** Sustainable investment refers to the selection of assets that contribute in some way to a sustainable economy, i.e., an asset that minimizes natural and social resource depletion. It is a broad term that may be used for the consideration of typical ESG issues and may include best-in-class. It can also include ESG integration, which considers how ESG issues impact a security's risk and return profile."
>
> —CFA Institute, "Certificate in ESG Investing: Official Training Manual," 3rd Edition, 2021

Provision 3.B.4

The INVESTMENT MANAGER SHOULD provide a definition for the terms "thematic" and "sustainable" the first time they appear in an ESG DISCLOSURE STATEMENT.

Discussion

The investment manager is encouraged to use one of the definitions previously referenced or a definition provided by an established standard setter or industry body. An investment manager may also choose to provide its own definition, in which case the definition should be consistent with the previously referenced definitions.

Sample Disclosure

"Sustainability is an important consideration for the ABC Growth and Income Fund. ABC Fund Management defines sustainability as the responsible and efficient consumption and management of natural resources that allow future generations to meet their own needs."

Impact Investing

References

> "**Impact Investing:** Impact investing refers to investments made with the specific intent of generating positive, measurable social and environmental impact alongside a financial return (which differentiates it from philanthropy)."
>
> —CFA Institute, "Certificate in ESG Investing: Official Training Manual," 3rd Edition, 2021

> "**Impact investments:** Impact investments are investments made with the intention to generate positive, measurable social and environmental impact alongside a financial return."
>
> —Global Impact Investing Network, "What You Need to Know about Impact Investing," 2021

> "**Impact investing:** Investing to achieve positive, social and environmental impacts—requires measuring and reporting against these impacts, demonstrating the intentionality of investor and underlying asset/investee, and demonstrating the investor contribution."
>
> —GSIA, "Global Sustainable Investment Review 2020," 2020

> "**Community investing:** Where capital is specifically directed to traditionally underserved individuals or communities, as well as financing that is provided to businesses with a clear social or environmental purpose. Some community investing is impact investing, but community investing is broader and considers other forms of investing and targeted lending activities."
>
> —GSIA, "Global Sustainable Investment Review 2020," 2020

Provision 3.B.5

The INVESTMENT MANAGER SHOULD use the term "impact investments" (and its variants) in a manner consistent with the previously referenced definitions.

Discussion

Provision 2.A.19 requires that if an investment product's investments are made with the intention to generate positive, measurable social and environmental impact alongside a financial return, then the investment manager must include certain disclosures in its ESG Disclosure Statement for that investment product. The intention to attain a positive, measurable social and environmental impact alongside a financial return is often referred to as impact investing. If an investment manager uses the term "impact investing," or one of its variants, in an ESG Disclosure Statement, it should do so in a manner consistent with the previously referenced definitions.

An investment manager should not use the term "impact investing" or its variants to refer to investing in companies with positive social or environmental characteristics that are doing "business as usual" when there is no intention to create a specific, measurable change or outcome in a social or environmental issue through an investment product's investments or stewardship activities. When describing the investment approach of investing in companies with positive social or environmental characteristics without an intention to attain a positive, measurable social or environmental change or outcome, the investment manager should consider the applicability of the following provisions:

- 2.A.9, Screening;
- 2.A.11, Portfolio-Level ESG Characteristics; or
- 2.A.14, Portfolio-Level Allocation Targets.

Provision 3.B.6

The INVESTMENT MANAGER SHOULD provide a definition for the term "impact" (and its variants) and the term "impact investments" (and its variants) the first time either term appears in an ESG DISCLOSURE STATEMENT.

Discussion

The investment manager is encouraged to use one of the definitions previously referenced or a definition provided by an established standard setter or industry body. An investment manager may also choose to provide its own definition, in which case the definition should be consistent with the previously referenced definitions.

Sample Disclosure for Provisions 3.B.5 and 3.B.6

"The BCD Biodiversity Fund (the 'Fund') was created to help prevent biodiversity loss in critical habitats and ecosystems in South America through direct debt and equity investments. Through its impact investments,[a] the Fund seeks to contribute to UN Sustainable Development Goal 15: *Protect, restore and promote sustainable use of terrestrial ecosystems, sustainably manage forests, combat desertification, and halt and reverse land degradation and halt biodiversity loss.*

[a] **Impact investments:** Impact investments are investments made with the intention to generate positive, measurable social and environmental impact alongside a financial return. (Global Impact Investing Network, 'What You Need to Know about Impact Investing,' 2021)"

Provision 3.B.7

The INVESTMENT MANAGER SHOULD NOT describe an INVESTMENT PRODUCT as having a positive ENVIRONMENTAL or SOCIAL impact if there is not at least a significant allocation to "impact investments" as defined by the previously referenced definitions.

Discussion

The investment manager is responsible for determining what proportion of a portfolio constitutes a significant allocation to impact investments. When determining whether an allocation is significant, the investment manager should consider whether the impact investments constitute the majority of the investment product's investments. Provision 2.A.19.f requires an investment manager to disclose the proportion of the portfolio that is allocated to impact investments.

Sample Disclosure

"The BCD Biodiversity Fund intends to invest the entirety of the Fund's £125M of committed capital in direct equity and debt in enterprises that provide solutions to protect and restore fragile ecosystems and habitats through sustainable forestry and land management practices."

ERRATA FOR THE EXPLANATION OF THE PROVISIONS OF THE GLOBAL ESG DISCLOSURE STANDARDS FOR INVESTMENT PRODUCTS

The following item reflects a correction to the Explanation of the Provisions of the Global ESG Disclosure Standards for Investment Products. Updated errata will be published on the ESG Disclosure Standards webpage hosted by CFA Institute.

Provision 2.A.8

If the INVESTMENT PRODUCT uses an ESG INDEX as an investment universe, then the INVESTMENT MANAGER MUST disclose:

a. either the significant ESG characteristics of the index or, if the index is a readily recognized index, the name of the index.

Sample Disclosure 2

"The XYZ Climate Index ('Index') is compatible with a 1.5-degree Celsius global warming climate scenario through the selection and weighting of its constituent securities. The Index is a subset of the XYZ Broad Market Equity Index. ~~The Index is designed to meet the minimum standards for methodology of an 'EU Paris-Aligned' benchmark.~~ The Index places a limit on exposure to companies that do not disclose their carbon emissions and applies constituent weighting caps to limit the Index's exposure to the physical and transition risks of climate change. The Index is constructed to have lower measures of greenhouse gas emissions and fossil fuel reserves than the XYZ Broad Market Equity Index. All Index constituents must be aligned with a transition pathway toward a 1.5-degree Celsius climate warming scenario. The Index excludes companies that generate revenue from coal, oil, or natural gas exploration or processing."

Made in United States
North Haven, CT
06 November 2026

21876159R00076